OCCASIONAL PAPER

55

PRODUCT QUALITY
PRODUCTIVITY
AND COMPETITIVENESS

A study of British and German ceramic tableware industries

NATIONAL INSTITUTE OF
ECONOMIC AND SOCIAL RESEARCH

OFFICERS OF THE INSTITUTE

PRESIDENT
SIR BRIAN CORBY

COUNCIL OF MANAGEMENT
J.S. FLEMMING (CHAIRMAN)

DIRECTOR
MARTIN WEALE

SECRETARY
GILL CLISHAM

2 DEAN TRENCH STREET, SMITH SQUARE, LONDON SW1P 3HE

PRODUCT QUALITY
PRODUCTIVITY
AND COMPETITIVENESS

A study of British and German ceramic tableware industries

VALERIE JARVIS

MARY O'MAHONY

AND HANS WESSELS

NATIONAL INSTITUTE OF ECONOMIC AND SOCIAL RESEARCH

PUBLISHED BY THE NATIONAL INSTITUTE
OF ECONOMIC AND SOCIAL RESEARCH
2 Dean Trench Street, Smith Square, London SW1P 3HE

First published 2002

Printed in Great Britain

A catalogue record of this book is available from the British Library

ISBN 0 9526213 9 8

Contents

Acknowledgements

We are grateful, above all, to the many manufacturers and buyers, who kindly gave their time to help and inform this study, and without whose insights and candour this paper could not have been written. Much additional helpful information and comment was received from others to whom thanks are due, in particular: In Britain (in chronological order): Kevin Farrell, British Ceramics Confederation; Seija Aalto, Sally Alsop, John Burnett and Ian Campbell, CERAM Research; Keith Marsh, Association for Ceramic Training and Development; Lorraine Ford, Retail Consortium; David Sanderson, School of Art and Design, Staffordshire University. In Germany: Lutz Graser, Verband der keramischen Industrie; Drs Nitsche, Bothner and their staff, Staatliches Berufsbildungszentrum für Keramik; Hubert Kittel, Faculty of Design, Hochschule für Kunst und Design, University of Halle; Walter Grottkopp, Hauptverband des Deutschen Einzelhandels.

We are grateful also to the Industry Economics and Statistics Directorate of the Department of Trade and Industry, for their generous financial support and many helpful comments during the project. The paper has benefited also from comments and insights from our colleagues at the National Institute. Particular thanks are due to our former colleague, Robert Anderton, for his contribution in the early stages of this project, and for comments on earlier drafts; to Sig Prais for suggestions and valuable advice throughout and to Micela Vecchi for assistance in some of the fieldwork. The authors alone are responsible for errors and omissions.

Addresses for correspondence: VJ & MO'M at National Institute of Economic & Social Research, 2 Dean Trench Street, Smith Square, London SW1P 3HE; HW at Deutsches Institut für Wirtschaftsforschung, Königin-Luise-Straße 5, 14195 Berlin.

Foreword

It is a privilege and a pleasure for me to contribute a foreword to this study. The DTI supported this study because, for all that is said and written about competitiveness, there are very few direct and concrete comparisons of the performance of British producers and of their principal competitors. Secondly, although *product quality* is central to competitiveness and wealth creation, it is paid less attention that it deserves because a product's quality depends upon a range of attributes (technical, practical and aesthetic) and is thus hard to measure. The study goes to the heart of what competitiveness is about: what do British and German companies actually produce? How does the average quality of their products compare? How and why are their products different? How much of the productivity gap does this quality differential help to explain? And, how are these quality differences achieved?

Answers to such questions are not to be found in comparisons of official statistics or company reports, but by methodical fieldwork on a consistent basis across countries. This is a most demanding type of research: it requires tact and persistence to secure the co-operation of many companies, the observational skills to piece together accurate pictures of two industries' products and production methods, and the analytical skills to interpret the findings. That is what the authors of this study have contributed in this study.

The tableware industry was chosen for comparison, not because it was thought that the industry performs badly in comparison with other UK manufacturing industries. On the contrary, it was considered important to study a UK industry which performs reasonably well. As the study makes clear, the British tableware industry does perform relatively well; it is one of the two most important ceramics industries in Europe, along with its German counterpart, and with a better export performance (higher exports and better balance of trade) than the latter.

The study offers insights into the UK's ways of organising its factories, education and training. It will be of interest to many outside the ceramics industry itself, including economic journalists, academics, think tanks and policy-makers. The study plays directly to the policy agenda of successive

British governments. As a recent White Paper on Enterprise, Skills and Innovation noted:

"UK productivity, however measured, lags behind that of other industrialised countries. The challenge for the Government is to achieve its long-term economic ambition to have a faster rise in productivity than its main competitors and so close that gap" (*Opportunity for all in a world of change*, Executive Summary, paragraph 5, February 2001).

This study demonstrates that, in this industry at least, differences in product quality explain a significant part of the UK-Germany productivity gap. Closing the gap, this study suggests, requires a wholesale reconsideration of the nature of the UK's long-standing skills deficiencies.

Nicholas Owen

Nicholas Owen
Director, Industry Economics and Statistics Directorate
Department of Trade and Industry

1

Introduction

The determinants of cross-country differences in economic performance have been much described, but remain ill-understood. In recent years, much effort has been expended by economists to seek to incorporate measures of relative product quality in cross-country comparisons as a means of explaining differences in performance between industrialised economies. Traditional approaches to incorporating qualitative elements – largely carried out by macroeconomists - rely, by necessity given the degree of aggregation of the data used, on proxy measures deemed responsible for quality differences (most commonly, expenditure on R&D) in seeking to explain cross-country differences in performance.[1] This project meanwhile, builds on the considerable experience of the NIESR team in carrying out detailed case-study analysis, based on visits to matched manufacturing plants in Britain and Germany, with a view to recording, for the industry in question, (a) whether a significant difference exists between the two countries in the *average* quality of total production; and (b) to examine in detail the factors – from raw materials to workforce skills – which contribute to those quality differences.[2]

The sector chosen for detailed study is that of the ceramic tableware industry. In keeping with the research brief agreed with our sponsors, the Industry Economics & Statistics Directorate of the UK Department of Trade nd Industry, this inquiry is therefore both broad in scope, reporting on a wide range of issues of relevance to discussions of UK industrial competitiveness, and deep in approach, concentrating on evaluating quality differences in a closely-defined group of products. The study includes detailed comparisons of real productivity – that is, adjusted for average quality of output – across a matched sample of tableware manufacturing plants in Britain and Germany. Estimates of real output per head from our sample plants are compared with aggregate comparisons (based on each country's Census of Production). The results are decomposed into volume and quality elements in an attempt to get a clearer notion of the nature and source of the noted German advantage.

The remainder of this report is set out as follows: Chapter 2 sets out the rationale for the selection of the sector, its appropriateness as an illustration of similar - mature - industries, and presents the underlying data based on published national statistics. Chapter 3 explores the principal quality features which distinguish the various 'quality-grades' of tableware, and summarises our work on quality differences in the two countries' consumption patterns. Chapter 4 looks at production in the two countries. We describe our case-study sample and its representativeness. In comparing productivity across the two countries, we seek to decompose the 'raw' productivity index into quantitative and qualitative aspects. Chapter 5 outlines the main differences in physical capital found in our samples of plants across the two countries. Chapter 6 deals with labour differences – from deployment to skills - in the principal activities of the manufacturing sector. Chapter 7 examines the differences in strategy we found from our discussions with manufacturers in Britain and Germany, and examines briefly the future prospects for the industry. Chapter 8 summarises the main results of this inquiry, and sets out the policy implications.

Notes

[1] See, for example: B Anderton, Innovation, Product Quality, Variety and Trade Performance: An Empirical Analysis of Germany and the UK, *Oxford Economic Papers*, 51 (1999), pp. 152-67.

[2] In a first empirical attempt to investigate whether, and if so how, the quality of manufactured goods varies in a systematic way between industrialised countries, Jarvis and Prais (1997) set about a detailed cross-country comparison of quality features and their impact on real productivity estimates for a range of three carefully-defined consumer products in Britain and Germany. That study, based on factory visits and discussions with industry experts in the two countries, showed a substantial German quality premium – of the order of 65 per cent above Britain – for the three products under consideration (blouses, secateurs, biscuits), and subsequent adjustments to national productivity estimates suggesting an average *real* (quality-adjusted) German productivity advantage over Britain of around 50 per cent for manufacturing as a whole. The study found two broad aspects of workforce skills particularly important in contributing to the higher-quality production observed: namely, skills relevant at the 'design interface' which helped German producers to develop new products and enter into new market areas, with production capabilities in mind; and the skills relevant to small- and medium-sized 'batch production' enabling quick and efficient changeover between smaller batches of semi-customised lines of the specialised varieties increasingly desired by consumers. (V Jarvis & SJ Prais, The quality of manufactured products in Britain and Germany, *International Review of Applied Economics* 11 (3), 1997, pp. 421-38.) The current study examines whether such finding hold for the ceramic industry, and provides greater detail on the 'mechanics' - and implications - of such differences on production capabilities.

2

The tableware sector in Britain and Germany

As an industry for study, the tableware sector offers a potentially interesting example of a mature industry, where production technologies and processes are largely known, and in which labour costs have been progressively reduced through specialisation and capital investment. The industry has successfully survived a range of perceived threats over the post-war period – from worries about the extent of competition (and potential substitution) from new substances (such as plastic) in the early post-war period, to more recent concerns regarding the trends towards less formal dining (or, as is often suggested, living!) arrangements, which have helped reduce demand for formal dinnerware.[3] Certainly, in the domestic sector, the tableware market is highly cyclical, in that its purchase can be easily postponed in times of economic hardship, and this, together with more casual dining trends, has led to some difficulties on the part of European manufacturers in recent years.[4] But it is the growth in external competition – particularly from lower-cost suppliers – that have generated the greatest causes for concern, and the most pressing needs to revise production strategies.

Despite these pressures, the two countries selected for comparison remain the two largest single tableware producers in Europe. And the sector is one in which Britain continues to fare relatively well in comparison to Germany – both in terms of employment and trade performance (see Table 1). Official figures for 1998 show total output in the household ceramics industry to be around 20 per cent higher in Britain than in Germany at market exchange rates, and employment around 25 per cent higher. On crude measures of output per employee, therefore, there appears little difference in the average productivity of labour in the two countries.[5]

Export activity is increasingly important for both countries, with exports now worth around £300 million annually and accounting for roughly half of total domestic production in both countries. In relative terms, however, the UK continues to fare rather better than Germany, with net exports of around £120 million each year, compared to a slight trade deficit (of £17 million) for Germany. For both countries, principal export markets are largely other

Table 1: Summary data on national household ceramics industries (SIC$_{92}$ 2621): Britain and Germany, 1998

	UK	Germany [a]	Ratio(UK=100)
Output (turnover, £m)	708.6	597.0	84
Employment (000s)	20,800	16,488	79
Output/employee (£)	34,067	36,207	106
Value-added per employee (£)	19,150	20,176	105
Exports (£m)	329.6	285.8	..
Imports (£m)	207.8	302.7	..
Trade Balance (£m)	121.8	-16.9	..
Export ratio (%) [b]	47	48	..
Import penetration (%) [c]	36	49	..

.. not applicable

[a] Converted at 2.914 DM/£ (Annual average of Bank of England monthly averages for 1998).

[b] Exports expressed as a percentage of total domestic production.

[c] Imports as share of total domestic demand.

Sources: for UK: ONS, *PRA 27 Household and Miscellaneous Ceramics*, 1998; unpublished data from Annual Employment Survey, 1998; ONS, *Annual Census of Production, 1998*; for Germany: Statistisches Bundesamt, *Produzierendes Gewerbe Fachserie 4 Reihe 4.1.1 Beschäftigung, Umsatz und Energieversorgung der Unternehmen und Betriebe im Bergbau und im verarbeitenden Gewerbe, 1998; Ibid., Produzierendes Gewerbe Fachserie 4 Reihe 4.3 Kostenstruktur der Unternehmen des Verarbeitenden Gewerbes sowie des Bergbaus und der Gewinnung von Steinen und Erden, 1998*; international trade: OECD, *International Trade by Commodities Statistics, Revision 2, 1990-1999*; Exchange rate published in Bank of England, *FinStats* (Sept 2000), Table 7.1A.

established industrialised countries with high levels of disposable income. But there are notable differences in the 'mix' of countries forming the major markets, with the US by far the largest single customer for the UK (alone accounting for over a quarter of total UK tableware exports), and just under 40 per cent of total exports going to the various neighbouring countries of the EU. Exports to Germany account for around 5 per cent of the British total.

For Germany, the remaining EU countries represent the major export market, accounting for some 55 per cent of export sales. The largest single market for German manufacturers of tableware is Italy, which alone imports roughly a quarter of that EU total; Austria, Belgium, France and the Netherlands are also important customers. Exports to Britain account for less than 4 per cent of total German tableware trade.[6]

While both countries rely heavily on imports from South East Asia (especially Taiwan, South Korea and China – particularly to satisfy the cheaper end of the ceramics market for, say, earthenware, stoneware, etc), similarly developed economies (particularly France, Portugal, Italy and – for the UK, at least - Japan) remain more important sources of supply for both countries. In 1998, imports from Asian countries represented about 45% of total UK imports and 30% of German imports; far more important for Germany was the Czech Republic (roughly 20 per cent of the total); while some 16 per cent of imports into Britain originated in Portugal. For sources, and a fuller breakdown of trade flows, see Appendix A.

Perhaps the greatest difference between the two countries' tableware markets lies in the form – that is, body paste - of tableware typically produced and consumed (see Table 2). Over 90 per cent of German tableware output is comprised of fine, high-value, porcelain - a product in which Germany's reputation has continued to grow ever since Böttger's discoveries in the early eighteenth century.[7] British tableware output, meanwhile, is more evenly divided between the production of porcelain (including the quintessentially English 'soft paste' porcelain derivative of bone china) which accounts for roughly 44 per cent of UK production, and the lower value (and less technically demanding) ceramics made from earthenware and stoneware (55 per cent of total UK output value).

These large differences in output-mix reflect - to some extent - differences in consumption patterns in the two countries. The Germans buyer's predilection for porcelain is apparent, to the extent that about 80 per cent of the value of tableware sales are constituted by sales of porcelain. In the formal dinnerware market, the average British consumer traditionally prefers the translucent finish of bone china. For everydayware - as well as, undoubtedly, for the more fashion- or price-conscious consumer, - earthenware remains an acceptable medium in the UK (accounting for approximately 45 per cent of UK sales in 1998), in stark contrast to the revealed preferences of German consumers. In addition, British consumers show a somewhat greater preference for stoneware, which has become increasingly fashionable in recent years.

Succinct as Table 2 may appear, two aspects of this table require further consideration: Firstly, it should be noted that these figures relate to total *values* of sales - *not* volumes (ie, units) of output produced for each of the categories. As such, they tell us little about the average values of individual pieces produced – either in each of the various categories, or in terms of the

5

Table 2: Consumption and production of tableware by body paste: Britain and Germany, 1998 (% total value of sales)

	Porcelain & bone china	Earthenware	Stoneware	Common pottery
Production				
UK	43.6	46.4	8.8	1.2
Germany	93.5	3.7	2.4	0.4
Consumption				
UK	42.0	45.0	11.6	1.4
Germany	81.5	9.5	7.2	1.8

Sources: for the UK: ONS, *PRA27 Household & Miscellaneous Ceramics, Product Sales and Trade, Ceramic Household and Ornamental Articles, 26210* (1999); for Germany: Eurostat, *Europroms: European Production and Market Statistics, 1998* (2nd edition).

'median' unit produced in each country. Secondly, the four categories for which these national distributions are available, distinguish between types of tableware production in terms of *physical* compositions alone: porcelain and bone china; earthenware; stoneware; and 'common pottery'.[8] The broad nature of the categories used means that – particularly in the relatively large categories of earthenware for the UK and porcelain for Germany - many different *qualities* of product are captured.

The definitions employed in describing physical composition themselves offer little insight into the important issue of relative output qualities. For instance, while bone china remains a relatively tight European standards-based definition (ie, requiring a bone ash content of *at least* 50 per cent in the raw clay mix), other categories are less well-defined: The term porcelain, for instance, is largely limited to that mix of clays and feldspar which yields a very low porosity after the high temperature first firing. Earthenware, meanwhile, consists of a broad 'catch all' category, covering a range of material mixes and subsequent body qualities from the most basic everydayware of 'once fired' earthenware, through its various derivatives (standard earthenware, faience, majolica, etc), to the daintiest vitrified 'fine china' formalware. To make the point at its most basic, under these categorisations, a raw clay mix containing 49 per cent bone ash content would here be classified to the category of earthenware, *not* bone china. The question of crucial importance to commentators and policy-makers interested in explaining cross-country differences in patterns of specialisation thus requires a rather greater understanding of the salient features defining tableware quality, and estimates as to the magnitude of any significant differences between the countries in the average quality of total production. These are the issues to which we now turn.

Notes

[3] According to some industry commentators, the trend towards less formal living arrangements – in particular, the trend reduction in the number of marriages – has had a dramatic effect on the industry, by substantially reducing demand for the industry's output! (See, for example: *Keynote Plus 1998 China and Earthenware*, p. 7.)

[4] Yet such trends offer new opportunities too: as incomes – and subsequent expenditure on leisure activities – rise, the growth in casual dining has been accompanied by an increased propensity to 'dine out', with an accompanying increase in demand for institutional tableware.

[5] Some adjustment should perhaps be made for typical differences in hours worked across the countries, since average annual hours worked tend to be lower in German manufacturing than in Britain. Estimates for total non-metallic mineral products suggest German employees work around 5% fewer hours per year in that sector, suggesting a raw productivity differential of around 10 per cent in Germany's favour. (See: M O'Mahony, *Britain's Relative Productivity Performance, 1950-1996: An International Perspective*. London: National Institute of Economic and Social Research, 1999). Part-time workers comprise a relatively small proportion of total employment in the tableware industry, only 4.3% of workers in the UK in 1998 (comparable figures for Germany were not available). Out-workers are an important labour input, however; but these are not included in national employment totals for the industry. Employment figures for the plant-level analysis carried out in Chapter 4, however, do include counts of temporary workers and out-workers in employment totals.

[6] Differences are also observable in terms of the mix of output sold abroad – with a considerably higher proportion of total German exports composed of the higher values goods, made from porcelain and bone china, which accounts for around 90 per cent of German exports, but only about 30 per cent of British tableware sold abroad; the larger component in British tableware exports is derived from the sale of earthenware (over 55 per cent).

[7] There remains some dispute between the countries as to the original inventor of European porcelain: Rosenthal notes a patent application lodged by the British potter, John Dwight, in 1671 - almost 40 years before the well-known German ceramicist, Johann Böttger, made his discovery. But Dwight's patent related to the development of what is known as *soft paste* porcelain, whereas Böttger succeeded in making the white translucent hard porcelain of a quality comparable to that previously imported – in some quantities – from the Far East. See: E Rosenthal, *Pottery and Ceramics* (Pelican, 1949; revised edition, 1954), pp. 36-7. For a fascinating, and eminently readable, account of Böttger's discoveries, see: J Gleeson, *The Arcanum: The Extraordinary True Story of the Invention of European Porcelain* (London: Bantum, 1998).

[8] The term 'common pottery' refers largely to the unglazed and more porous wares, such as terracotta.

3

Assessing quality in tableware

W hile the choice of sector – tableware – was deliberately made in order to keep the central quality elements of the study within manageable constraints, a word needs to be said about the operational means of assessing the overall 'quality' of the output of a sector in which value is added not just in terms of technical functionality (use, 'washability', impact resistance, etc), but equally by dint of enhanced shape, style, decoration, after-sales service (including repeats, replacements), etc. To this extent a formal, classic bone china or porcelain dinner service may cost hundreds of pounds, while a simple – often imported – earthenware set retails at less than £20. In assessing the quality of the end product, a method needed to be devised which enables account to be taken of the full range of both the technical qualities of the product, as well as considered views as to the more subjective, but nevertheless market-friendly, features embodied in the end product.

Since for most individuals, the purchase of a quality dinner service is a relatively rare – often, once-in-a-lifetime – event, their lack of 'dimensions experience' (that is, of repeat purchasing, especially at the higher quality grades) makes it difficult to gain a very considered opinion as to the relative merits of a given manufacturer over others from that source. Similarly, it would be unwise to seek information from manufacturers alone. To overcome these difficulties, therefore, in addition to the views of manufacturers, we sought the views of a handful of experienced tableware buyers from leading retailers (6 in the UK, 5 in Germany) in the two countries, capable of assessing (often in retrospect) the relative qualities of domestically-bought tableware ranges, and able to comment in detail on the principal distinctions and similarities in the tastes and tendencies of the UK and German tableware-buying public.[9]

To aid our 'panel' in their task, it was necessary that the product under discussion was sufficiently similar so as to be able to focus the discussion around the inherent aspects of a piece of tableware which contributed to its overall quality and saleability. To this end, we selected one of the most widely-produced items within most manufacturers' product mix - a 26/27 cm dinner plate – for comparison.[10]

3.1 Quality attributes

The humble dinner plate is not all it seems: many features contribute to the overall 'quality' of a plate – from the objective criteria of body paste, weight and finish, to the more subjective elements, such as style, shape and design. On the basis of our discussions with manufacturers and retail buyers in the two countries it seems that, despite the relatively unsophisticated nature of our product, certain aspects - not always immediately obvious to the ordinary consumer - are particularly important in assessing the overall quality of a given item of tableware. We next summarise these aspects - from materials to after-sales service, before considering the relative importance of these factors in differentiating tableware into distinct quality-grades.

Body paste
At the simplest level four broad categories of tableware can be distinguished according to raw materials involved: porcelain (composed of china clay, feldspar, and quartz); bone china (composed of at least 50% calcified animal bone, china stone and china clay); earthenware (china clay, ball clay, flint); and stoneware (similar to earthenware, but with a higher stone content and lower porosity). Both Britain and Germany produce and consume all varieties, though the shares of the various types in national totals vary considerably, as discussed in Chapter 2.

In terms of technical attributes, European standards for impact resistance ('breakability') of tableware do not exist, while the existing EU standards on detergent resistance ('washability') are currently under review. And a cursory examination of a plate - by reading information printed on its base - tells us little about these attributes.

The choice of paste used has important implications for the functionality of tableware: the harder bodies of say, porcelain and bone china, make for greater impact (ie, drop and chip) resistance in use, compared to the softer-paste earthenware fired at lower temperatures. Moreover, the choice of paste may impart improved manufacturing properties (eg, greater stability during firing; reduction in necessary numbers of firings, say 'once-fired earthenware') or additional qualities of interest to the end-user (for instance, enhanced heat retention, especially important for institutional caterers).

While the German consumer remains heavily committed to porcelain, most of the UK experts suggested that the typical British consumer is largely unaware of the greater durability of porcelain in comparison to earthenware. However, there is evidence that consumers in the UK are increasingly aware of the negative aspects of earthenware – that is, its propensity to chip – and some of this recognition helps to explain the rather increased demand for the more durable alternative of stoneware.[11]

Glazing

The type of body paste used, and the degree and form of decoration subsequently applied, have important implications for the type and form of glazing typically carried out across firms. In determining the decorating process, each manufacturer needs, for instance, to decide whether to substitute a greater range of ceramic colours available for in- and on-glaze decoration requiring a lower temperature firing (or perhaps tolerate a potentially higher rate of rejects and seconds due to colour-distortion during firing) with the harder finish and less permeable 'under-glaze' decoration. The final choice of glaze in turn brings implications for the colour-fastness and detergent-resistance of the decoration, as well as the 'robustness' of the glaze itself (ability to withstand scratching, crazing, etc). Glaze ingredients, and their cost, vary across manufacturers.

According to our experts, faultless glazing is a particularly important determinant of overall quality of tableware, since the customer can – to some extent – see and feel where glazing is not good. From our manufacturers' samples, it seemed that, on everydayware at least, this aspect was afforded rather more attention in Germany.

Design and decoration

The nature and degree of embellishment, it is universally acknowledged, plays a key role in determining commercial success of the various tableware ranges in this increasingly design-conscious sector. Here it seems, the British and German tableware-buying public have historically exhibited differing tastes in buying patterns, with the British preferring, on the whole, more heavily patterned and decorated tableware compared to the plainer, often completely unembellished 'whitewares' typically purchased in Germany.[12] Such differences in consumer preferences can be expected to have an impact on the mix of domestic output. Differences in preferences aside, three design features in particular were felt to contribute particularly to the overall quality - and saleability - of a given product. In brief:

- *colour:* Experts in both countries suggested any colour applied as a design was perhaps the single most important factor influencing purchasing decisions – to the extent that 'getting the colour wrong' resulted in significantly reduced sales;
- *structural form:* While variation in shape is less pronounced in plates and other flatware, variations are noticeable– for instance, in depth (with extremes of almost flat to bowl-like appearance); in shape (eg, round, oval, square or geometric); and in the uniformity of depth (eg, whether a plate slopes towards the centre, or has a distinctly raised rim). While a variety of all of these shapes could be found in both countries, it seems that the higher predilection for whitewares in Germany makes structural form a somewhat greater consideration than in Britain;
- *surface decoration:* This was perhaps the most subjective – and difficult – area for all the participants in our study; and cross-country differences in tastes play an important role in the market for tableware in the two countries.

While undecorated whiteware is currently in vogue in both countries, it remains much more of a staple in the German market than in Britain; on the whole, it seems, British consumers tend to prefer a rather more decorated plate. Demand is thus greater in the UK for bolder, starker patterns, with British consumers more likely to buy heavily decorated, often gilded, designs. The typical German consumer tends to prefer a more simply decorated product – with less gilding, preferring instead as formal ware a higher grade, finer, lighter and 'whiter' porcelain product - with little (if any) applied decoration other, perhaps, than an embossed surface pattern.

Finishing

The method used – hand decoration, spray, lithographed transfer, etc - to apply surface designs to a plate has important implications for costs of production, with more mechanised techniques costing less per unit than those which are highly labour intensive. While automated printing is now capable of applying relatively sophisticated patterns to plates, for higher quality products, the buyers we spoke to in both countries appeared to favour lithographic and hand-decoration techniques, because of the greater depth (more delicate designs, finer lines) and definition (a greater range of colours, sharper contrasts, etc) of finishing which they afforded.

Similarly, imperfections due to say, contamination by dust or colour leaching during firing, crazed glazing, offset decorations, unpolished rims, etc, all play a role in delineating the overall quality of a finished piece.

After-sales service

While ever more product ranges are deliberately designed with seasonal trends in mind, most manufacturers offer a core of long-standing 'classics', which have been marketed for decades or more. Among sales of high-value formalware in particular, the ability to re-order - for additions, replacements of broken items, etc – over some years is viewed as a key element of customer service and product quality in the eyes of the consumer. From our wider discussions with buyers and retail staff in the two countries, it appears that this aspect is afforded rather more priority in Britain than Germany, where only the very highest range items are typically sold with a minimum reordering guarantee.

For most manufacturers in both countries, the 'customer' is somewhat removed from the end-user of the tableware, in that most producers supply first to a wholesaler or retailer who in turn supplies the domestic or institutional customer. Yet the ability to 'give customers what they want' and *timed to fit* in with say, seasonal or promotional events is a topic of continual irritation among buyers in both countries. As transport costs and times diminish, a key advantage of the European producers over their further-flung competitors - that of reacting first to changes in consumer demand - requires ever-faster reaction times. Experts suggested that British manufacturers have tended to be notably slower at satisfying customer orders and repeats than their German counterparts - to the extent, we were told, that stock turnover rates for most UK firms currently average only 2-3 times per year, compared to 5-6 times a year for most German producers.[13]

3.2 How well do prices reflect product quality?

From an economic perspective, we might expect that the various quality dimensions outlined above should have some impact on the price at which each product sells in the market. Clearly an elaborately decorated bone china plate with a gilded rim sells for a considerably higher price than a plain white earthenware plate, not least since the production of the former involves a more complex and costly process. Since a key objective of the current project was to quantify differences in the average quality of output in the two countries, we sought to examine to what extent differences in average output quality might be reasonably approximated by differences in price. Our investigations thus included a series of analyses using the standard economist's tool of hedonic regression techniques as a means of examining the explanatory power of price as a proxy for quality.

Hedonic regression analysis

This approach involved the careful scrutiny and detailed recording of both quality dimensions and prices for a broad sample of dinner plates collected from a range of retail outlets in Britain and Germany in November/December 1999 and Spring 2000. In total, some 282 plates were priced in Britain, and 145 in Germany, giving a combined sample of 427 plates.[14] The retail outlets chosen covered a wide range of plates from the very cheap to very expensive. The objective was to secure prices for as varied a selection of plates as possible, so as to enable sufficient variation within the sample for each quality dimension. This necessitated gathering data on prices of plates produced outside Britain and Germany, although production from these two countries alone constituted some 60% of the total sample. Sample details are provided in Appendix B.

The quality dimensions chosen for recording were guided by the discussions with buyers, as summarised above. The dimensions observed thus included a mixture of both objective characteristics (such as body paste, degree and mode of decoration, etc), as well as more subjective criteria related

13

to the market to which they are aimed (for instance, once-in-a-lifetime purchases, 'stylishness', etc).

Four categories of body paste were distinguished: earthenware; stoneware; porcelain; and bone china. A second basic distinction was that between whiteware and decorated plates. Within whitewares, we further distinguished between plain and embossed items. Within the decorated (ie, non-whiteware) sample, we recorded data at a number of levels. An initial distinction was made between those plates which were entirely one colour or included merely a single coloured band ('single design') and those with more elaborate designs involving several shades of a colour or multi-coloured designs ('multi-design'). For these decorated plates, we further differentiated those with gilding – that is, for our purposes, including some gold or other (semi-)precious metal. Finally, the method by which decorations were applied to the plate was also noted, with our sample divided between those that were: hand-decorated and/or colour-washed; decorated by lithographic transfer; or stamped (with the colour and/or design applied by machinery). Initially, our 'subjective' dimensions were limited to whether the plate was likely to be purchased for everyday use; because it was 'stylish'; or as a once-in-a-lifetime purchase – a division suggested on the basis of our discussions with experienced retail buyers.

Regression results

For computational purposes, these quality dimensions were transformed into a series of dummy variables taking the value of 1 if a plate exhibited a particular characteristic; 0 otherwise. The log of the price was regressed on these quality dummies, together with additional dummy variables representing the country in which the observations were recorded. In this formulation, the estimated coefficients on the quality dummies represent the proportionate amount by which price changes according to the characteristics included.

Table 3 presents the results of three of the specifications used for this regression analysis.[15] In the first specification - equation (1) - the results suggest that, all other things equal, in relation to an earthenware benchmark, a porcelain body adds about 50 per cent to price, whereas a bone china body doubles it. Hand decoration and transfer printing also add significantly to price, although by less than the body paste dimensions. The remaining variables shown have smaller impacts, and are not significant (95% confidence limit). These results seem highly plausible, but the variables included explain only around half of the variation in price of our sample (adjusted R^2 of 0.57).

Equation (2) adds the more subjective quality elements while omitting other variables such as 'white embossed', 'single colour' and 'multi' designs, whose significance were further reduced when these new variables were added. All variables have the expected (positive) sign, and are statistically significant. The proportionate impact on price of porcelain or bone china body paste are much reduced in this second equation, with high effects from the market to which they are aimed. The proportion of variation in price explained by the new equation now rises to around two-thirds (R^2 of 0.67).

Table 3: Hedonic regression results: Percentage addition to price by changes to characteristics over undecorated earthenware dinner plate

	Equation (1)	Equation (2)	Equation (3)
Stoneware	21	14	13
Porcelain	49	37	23
Bone China	105	68	41
White embossed	5	-	-
Single design	5	-	-
Multi-design	15	-	-
Gilded	11	4	10
Hand-decorated	45	24	31
Litho-transfer	36	27	25
Stylish	-	55	42
One-off purchase	-	75	55
International Brand Name	-	-	56
National Brand Name	-	-	48
Equation adjusted R^2	0.57	0.67	0.73

Figures derived from regression results (See: Table B.3)

Our discussions with retail buyers, meanwhile, had suggested that an important element in purchasing decisions was brand name, which might be viewed - in the eyes of consumers, at least – as a proxy for a range of quality dimensions, which our recordings could not easily quantify. Thus a second non-objective dimension was added to explanatory variables, by distinguishing within our sample of plates those produced by what might be termed 'household names', and those produced by other manufacturers. Within branded goods, we further distinguished two discrete groups; those plates produced by manufacturers with an *internationally* recognised brand name; and a second group of *national* brands, defined as products which were considered to command a price premium in one of the two countries, but were not regarded as branded goods in the other.[16] Both brand categories might be assumed to convey information on unobservable quality characteristics, but the international brand name appears also to capture some additional dimensions of desirability – perhaps the desire for 'exclusivity'.

Equation (3) thus includes the two brand variables. Both are statistically significant, with the international brand variable having, as might be expected, the greater impact on price variation. Certainly with these additional subjective variables (market segment *and* brand name) included, our model can be described – in statistical terms, at least – as offering a reasonable fit, with over 75 per cent of the variation in price explained by the characteristics included in the regressions.[17]

A useful output from this specification is that the ratio of the coefficient on the dummy variable for a plate sold in Germany to the coefficient on the corresponding UK dummy yields an estimated quality-standardised PPP of some 2.53 DM/£. In contrast to the very similar levels of output per employee estimated using market exchange in Chapter 1, using this standardised PPP exchange rate suggests a significant productivity advantage in Germany's favour (see below).

There are, however, a number of difficulties with the hedonic approach, since it relies heavily on the ability to quantify the various dimensions for analysis. Some quality dimensions are more easily observed than others, while characteristics such as functionality, glaze and finish are difficult to quantify within the limitations of a binary variable. In this analysis, we sought to deal with some of the difficulties by using brand names as proxies for the unquantifiable dimensions. While it seemed possible to explain around three-quarters of the variation in price, we did not feel that the price alone adequately estimated differences in output quality. And there remains little common agreement (even among the members of this team) as to what – from hidden quality indicators to degrees of market power – is actually being represented by variables such as brand names. A more important question, perhaps, is whether such a decomposition of the various individual elements which contribute to a good's overall quality is really a sufficient method for comparing output quality among manufacturers or countries. An alternative is to use a more direct approach – this is the method to which we now turn.

3.3 Quality equivalences

It is, of course, the particular *combination* of features which determines the overall quality of a given product. An alternative approach is therefore to seek to group products into *quality-equivalent* grades whilst taking account of the full range of quality attributes embodied in each product. The method has the advantage that even relatively rare specimens - with few direct matches – can be accommodated, since it is the overall *mix* of features which determines quality equivalence. For international comparisons, it has the advantage that differences in consumer tastes can be largely discounted, in that differences in preferences can be largely delineated into the underlying features that they reflect. It thus allows a comparison of products representative of the national market (or output) to be compared irrespective of whether that product would be likely to sell well in the second country, or not. Finally, this method enables a greater degree of differentiation between plates of ostensibly similar body pastes across a range of quality-grades – a feature of particular importance where the broad terms of earthenware and porcelain disguise a range of qualities of output (*cf.* discussion on p. 6, above).

Four quality grades
None of the manufacturers or retailers we spoke to were able to offer any kind of 'optimal mix' of characteristics which would clearly delineate a given plate to a particular grade. Nevertheless, most found it possible to agree on a combination of features which distinguished our sample plates – sourced from both 'domestic' (ie, German and British) suppliers *and* 'foreign' (ie, third-country) producers.[18]   Four 'rule of thumb' quality-grades were arrived at:
- *Top-quality* plates invariably denoted the highest grade formalware, made of bone china or very fine grade porcelain, decorated with an elegant surface pattern or embossed design, often with a degree of gilding. Most, we were told by our retail experts, would almost

exclusively be the stuff of wedding lists, with individuals themselves usually buying only single pieces to replace damaged or broken items. - *Superior* quality plates shared many of these characteristics, though to a lesser degree overall. The plates assessed here included both what might be categorised as high-grade everydayware, as well as more traditional wedding-list items. A major distinction between this and the above and lower categories had much to do with the body paste of the plates in question – our respondents being seemingly reluctant to categorise anything other (with one or two exceptions) than finest-grade porcelain and bone china, to the top quality grades. The exceptions were made for items deemed of such high quality in other aspects – perhaps due to an innovative design or shape - that their overall composition warranted inclusion in this 'superior quality' category.

- *Standard* quality plates included plates of porcelain, earthenware and stoneware, generally intended for everyday use, but lacking the refinements or originality of the higher grades.

- *Basic* quality plates were clearly lacking in at least one dimension. This included plate samples with poor coverage or 'crazing' of the glaze; pitted – 'orange peel' – surfaces; firing chips not ground down; or poor-quality copies of original designs. Functionally, the plates were usable but their durability was questionable.

For the sake of clarity, it is important to emphasise that the plates were allocated across the various grades according to their *combined* mix of physical and aesthetic attributes - *not* their price, *nor* brand. In fact, respondents were not told of the brand, origin or price of an item until they had assessed its quality features; any identifying features which might have been evident from the backstamp were carefully covered by a sticker denoting each plate merely with a code. Thus while almost all of the plates assigned to the top-quality grade emerged as branded goods by the well-known (international) producers, the brand name itself would not dictate entry into this category; and many of the branded pieces were placed in lower categories, based – quite properly in the spirit of the current investigation – solely on their mix of embodied and aesthetic characteristics.

Our final calculations were based on a sample of 28 plate samples in the top group, 31 in the superior group, 33 in the standard group and 23 in the basic group. Within these rankings, examples of porcelain tableware featured in each one of the quality-grades, earthenware in three of the four grades. Market prices for each of the sample plates in each grade were averaged, and combined with information on the quantity shares of total domestic sales in each category in the two countries, estimated on the basis of discussions with buyers, and supplemented with published reports on tableware markets (see Table 4).[19]

Table 4: Quality-equivalences, retail prices, market shares and PPP estimates

	Average retail prices			Average share of domestic sales(% volume)	
Quality grade	*UK*	*D (DM)*	*D (£)* [a]	*UK*	*D*
Top	21.42	47.25	15.90	10	20
Superior	11.33	25.41	8.55	30	40
Standard	7.31	16.29	5.48	30	25
Basic	3.01	8.23	2.77	30	15

Average price of fixed basket of qualities (weighted by shares of quality grades bought in UK, Germany)

	UK shares	German shares	Ratio D/UK
At UK prices	8.64	11.09	1.28
At German prices	6.63	8.39	1.26
Implied quality effect			
at 'common' prices	7.57	9.65	1.27 [b]
Price effect [c]	-30%	-32%	-31% [b]
Implied Purchasing Power Parity (PPP) exchange rate			
PPP	2.38	2.31	2.34 [b]

[a] Converted at 2.971 DM/£ (Mean of monthly Bank of England averages for 1999, taken from ONS, *Finstats*, Sept 2000, Table 7.1A).[b] Geometric mean.[c] Percentage differential in purchase price of fixed basket of qualities at German v. UK prices.

In looking simply at the typical retail prices paid by consumers in the two countries, it appears that there is little overall difference in the average qualities bought across the countries, since the average plate bought by German consumers in 1999 typically retailed at around 25 DM – equivalent to around £8.39 at market exchange rates, while the average plate bought in Britain cost around £8.64. But this similarity in the average price paid in the two countries conceals an important qualitative element. Looking at the distributions of sales by quality grades across the two countries shows that German consumers bought significantly more of the two higher quality grades (accounting for roughly 60 per cent of total items bought) than their British counterparts (roughly 40 per cent of sales). Measured in common prices, it seems, German consumers typically choose tableware items incorporating some 27 per cent higher quality attributes than their British peers. But average retail prices were around 30 per cent *lower* in Germany than in the UK *for equivalent quality-grades* (contrast the various national shares at UK versus German prices). Put simply, it seems, the German consumer *pays slightly less in nominal terms*, but gets a substantially *better product in real terms*.

According to these estimates, and based on the ratio of the (geometric) average across the prices in the two countries, the real purchasing-power-parity (PPP) exchange rates for tableware should be around 2.34 DM/£ - substantially below the 2.97 DM/£ nominal exchange rate for that year. It is particularly interesting to note that at the higher quality grades the differential is even greater – at around 2.23 DM/£.

Notes

[9] In addition, we gained valuable insights from a variety of technically-qualified personnel from the UK's leading standards testing agency, CERAM, as well as from extensive conversations with participants at the two major European trade fairs for tableware, held in Frankfurt in February and August 2000.

[10] Clearly the technical processes (and production costs) involved in moulding, firing, decorating and glazing of a relief-pressed jug or coffee pot - perhaps further embellished with transfer patterns or hand-finishing or gilding - differ considerably from the largely two-dimensional nature of the production of a standard undecorated white dinner plate. Nevertheless, to keep the *relative* assessments within manageable limits - not least, from the team's perspective, since these samples were physically carried from country to country - the choice of item is of lesser importance.

[11] One of the buyers we spoke to in the UK suggested that returns of earthenware products had become so acute that the chain has now abandoned earthenware entirely in favour of a mix of stoneware and porcelain products. A second suggested that their store would soon follow suit.

[12] Moreover, there appears to be a subtle difference between consumers in the two countries in their appreciation of the 'whiteness' of the background colour - with the British preferring a slightly 'yellower' or 'beiger' (according to the Germans) plate to the 'greyer' (according to the British) white associated with traditional European porcelain.

[13] The 'complacency' of both UK and German manufacturers in this instance is perhaps better understood, when one acknowledges that typical stock turnover rates among US and Japanese suppliers are widely held to be around 7 and 12 times a year, respectively!

[14] The unbalanced size of the sample in the two countries in part reflects the differing retail distribution systems in the two countries. Department stores are more prevalent in the UK, whereas German consumers are more likely to purchase these items from smaller specialist retailers (*Fachgeschäfte*). Since most (even major) cities in Germany typically support only a small number of such specialist shops (and each with a more limited range than is typically carried by the average department store), it was more difficult to obtain a large number of price quotations there.

[15] For a fuller elaboration of the sampling method, the distribution of our samples by quality dimensions, as well as further results, see Appendix B.

[16] We were informed in this process by our discussions with retail buyers.

[17] Additionally, we estimated equations allowing the characteristics to vary across the two countries by interacting the

quality characteristics with the German dummy variable. The results are presented in Table B.3 in Appendix B, where very insignificant interaction variables (with t-ratios less than 1) were omitted. Adding these variables only marginally increases the adjusted R^2. The coefficients on porcelain and bone china body pastes are negative and significant suggesting these two types of paste add proportionally less to price in Germany than in Britain when allowance is made for other variables. In fact the results suggest that a porcelain body, on its own, does not command a price premium in Germany (as might be expected in a country where porcelain is the standard medium for tableware), but that brand name commands a significantly greater premium in Germany than in Britain.

[18] The allocation of each plate into one of these four groups was based on the quality aspects delineated above on the basis of our discussions with retail buyers. Each buyer was shown a sample of plates, and asked to assign them to three or four (as they saw fit) distinct quality-grades according to each plate's overall combination of physical and aesthetic attributes. Given the nature of the product (its bulk and weight), it was not always possible to show the same full sample of plates to *all* buyers in *both* countries while ensuring a sufficiently large sample of representative examples from each country. The equivalences were therefore undertaken by the researchers using as our starting point the samples shown to one or more of our experts. The sample was then enhanced with further examples which typified the category based on the agreed quality features, as signalled by our experts. For each quality-grade, we divided between decorated and whiteware products. Input from the NIESR team was largely limited to seeking additional observations in the basic and whiteware categories in order to increase the sample size.

[19] The resulting price ratios were subjected to statistical tests to assess their robustness regarding the inclusion or deletion of individual plates, as well as for small changes in the weighting schemes, both overall categories and ratios of white to decorated plates. Despite the small sample sizes involved (for statistical tests of this type), the results were found to be reasonably robust: the overall German/UK price ratio did not change by more than 5% in any of the alternative specifications.

4

Productivity and quality: Case-study results

S o far, we have dealt only with sales; in particular, with the elucidation of the tendency for the average German consumer typically to select tableware which incorporates around one-third higher quality content than in Britain, together with a summary of the particular features which contribute to higher tableware quality from the perspective of the consumer. Such a result need not concern us unduly, so long as it is not similarly reflected in real differences in the quality-grades of tableware *produced* in the two countries.

The reputations of Britain's top tableware producers compare well with the best anywhere in the world; yet the extent to which these highly renowned manufacturers exemplify a *tendency* for high-quality production in the UK remains an empirical question. A key feature of the current study then, was to investigate the extent to which the *typical* British tableware manufacturer - and not simply those with vast financial resources and production potential at their disposal - possesses the skills, machinery and know-how necessary to be able to continue to produce for domestic and world markets in the face of growing international competition. As we shall demonstrate in what follows, from our plant-level observations and discussions with manufacturers, it seems that a markedly greater proportion of total production consists of higher quality grades in Germany than in Britain, and that this marked difference translates directly into a considerable real productivity advantage among German manufacturers.

4.1 The firm sample

The findings of this report are based in large part on detailed observation and discussion with a broad spectrum of tableware manufacturers in the two countries. All but one of the participating firms were visited by at least two of the NIESR team investigators. Discussions took the form of semi-structured interviews, involving questions ranging from basic data on levels of output and employment, to more detailed inquiries regarding the skill-levels and qualifications of production operatives, auxiliary workers and management; recent innovations in the production process; design and R&D capabilities. Somewhat unexpectedly - not least, in the light of the intense competition currently faced by the industry in both countries, - almost all of the firms approached (all but one in each country) agreed to participate, thanks largely, we suspect, to the help and advice of the relevant trade associations in each of the countries. Their executives helped guide us as to whom we might contact from the numerous companies registered as operating within the tableware sector, provided us with introductions to the firms visited, and offered insights into the typicality of each of the producers in national totals. In all but one (German) case, investigators also visited the production facilities of the sample companies, in order to gain a first-hand impression of differences in the scope and set-up of production facilities, labour input and deployment, and the type of output typically produced within the plant visited.

In total, our study involved visits and interviews to a total of 23 tableware manufacturing firms (12 in the UK, 11 in Germany) across the two countries, involving discussions with factory owners, production managers, and directors, whose firms between them represent over 20,000 employees across the two countries – equivalent to roughly half of total industry employment.[20] Since a key feature of the project was to report in detail on the differences in strategy, capacity and output quality across the two countries, and the issues faced by a 'typical plant' within the wider tableware industry, the generalisability of the results depends crucially on the degree to which the plants visited might be construed to be representative of the industry as a whole.

Table 5 summarises the size distribution of manufacturing plants visited in the course of this inquiry. In approaching the firms within our sample, we did not have precise information as to individual plant sizes. And attempts at systematic selection by means of a sampling frame have been further hampered both by the considerable degree of consolidation and rationalisation activity taking place within the tableware industries of both countries over the course of this study.[21] Moreover, it is not uncommon to find manufacturers organising the various production activities across several specialised sites, so that say, the forming and decorating activities may be spread among a number of manufacturing plants; or organising production of different types (eg, bone

23

china as opposed to earthenware) in different 'local units'. This complication means that while our sample consists of some 12 *firms* in Britain, and 11 in Germany, our discussions and observations took place in a range of some 17 separate *plants* in the UK, 13 in Germany.[22]

Table 5: Size distribution of sample plants visited: tableware, 1999-2000

	UK		Germany	
	No plants visited	% share of employment	No plants visited	% share of employment
<200	6	8	3	8
200-499	7	46	7	41
500+	4	45	3	50
	17	100	13	100
Total employment	5,260		4,541	
Plant average	309		349	

For comparisons with size distribution in national populations, and a further breakdown of the combined plant-level employment from each of firms visited, see Appendix C.

As it turned out, the average size of the plants that agreed to participate (in 1999-2000) are slightly lower than the most recent (1995) published medians for the industry as a whole, at 319 employees for the UK, 349 for Germany. This slight difference in average plant size between the countries need not concern the reader for two reasons. Firstly, in computing our cross-country productivity ratios, only the *combined* output and employment figures from each of the firms visited were used. (A similar breakdown of firm size on the basis of the combined employment for each of the plants visited per firm shows an even greater correspondence in average firm sizes, with employment averages per firm visited of 438 and 413 for the UK and Germany, respectively – see Appendix C.) Secondly, in a further effort to represent more closely the actual performance levels of the *national* industries, these figures were then weighted ('grossed up') in proportion to each firm's share of total domestic *tableware manufacturing* employment.[23] More importantly, however, not all of the firms visited were willing to provide the full range of data required to be included in all parts of the analysis, so that the productivity estimates that follow later in this chapter are based on weighted averages for 10 firms (12 plants) in Germany, 9 firms (12 plants) in the UK.

In terms of other attributes, some 10 of the 12 firms visited in our

British sample were located in and around the well-known 'Potteries' area of Stoke-on-Trent; 7 of our 11 firms in Germany were geographically clustered in traditional ceramics producing areas, centred on Selb in Oberfranken. Around half of our sample in each country were either private ('limited company') businesses or family concerns; half listed companies. Finally, while our intention in this study project was to focus on the *typical* producers of each country, in view of the very different historical specialisations in the form of output produced in the two countries – that is, Germany's noted heavy concentration in the production of porcelain, compared to the UK's dual focuses in the manufacture of ceramics made of both bone china and earthenware - special efforts were made to ensure that our sample also included manufacturers of comparable output types across the two countries. Thus in both countries, at least one visit was made to a producer for each of the four main body pastes (disclosure issues prevent further elaboration).

4.2 Productivity estimates: basic data

As outlined above, in the course of our case-study visits, we collected detailed information on output measures (value and volume produced; composition of output – flatware, whiteware, etc, as a share of total; where possible, value-added), and employment, decomposed into the various departments. Turnover figures were collected to relate solely to the plants visited. Raw data on employment figures were carefully adjusted to ensure comparability of numbers across the firms visited, and to ensure that part-time workers were counted only in relation to the fraction of a total working week actually worked. Since it is now common practice across a good many tableware manufacturers to 'outsource' many of the auxiliary functions to the manufacturing process – for instance, clay-making replaced by granulate, security and cleaning functions, etc - these workers were excluded from the employment totals for *all* of the firms visited (where necessary, employees' time was apportioned between activities). Employment totals for each plant were further adjusted to take account of temporary – often 'agency' – staff not officially on their books, but who nevertheless contribute to output. Where outsourcing of say, decorating activities took place, the employment totals of decorating departments were proportionally increased. Finally, apprentices spending, on average, only 3½ days per week in the company in Germany (the remaining day and a half being spent at vocational college – or its equivalent, in the form of *Blockunterricht*), were counted as the equivalent of 0.7 of a full-time worker. Bearing these refinements in mind, Table 6 summarises our productivity estimates for the sample plants visited in Britain and Germany.

Table 6: Productivity estimates for Britain and Germany from sample plants: 1999-2000

ALL EMPLOYEES	UK	Germany	Ratio UK=100
Turnover per employee (£000 pa)	42.2	54.8	130
Physical productivity (000 pieces pa)	32.8	22.7	69
Average unit value per piece produced (£)	1.29	2.41	188
Value-added per employee	22.8	30.8	135
DIRECT WORKERS			
Turnover per direct worker (£000 pa)	49.0	70.4	144
Volume per direct worker (000 pieces pa)	37.5	29.9	80

German figures converted at 2.917 DM/£ (average of Bank of England monthly averages).

As Table 6 shows, from our sample of manufacturing units, taking all employees together, the average value of sales per employee was some £55,000 in Germany, compared to £42,000 in the UK – an apparent German advantage of around 30 per cent. In terms of physical units produced, however, British manufacturers' output actually exceeds that of Germany, with each British employee typically producing some 33,000 pieces per year, on average, compared to 23,000 per employee in the average German plant. But there is an important difference in the value of the output produced. Valued at factory prices, each 'unit' of output produced in Germany typically comprises an altogether higher-value product (we refrain – deliberately - from the term 'higher quality'; that aspect will be explored below), with a unit value almost 90 per cent higher than that of the average piece produced in Britain.

Taking only 'direct' production workers into account – that is, ignoring for the moment those involved in managerial positions or as support staff, as well as the imputed proportions of head office personnel attributable to the factories in our sample, supervisory staff, those in maintenance, etc – our sample suggests an even greater (44 per cent) German advantage in terms of turnover per employee, together with a slight narrowing of the British physical advantage.

The production of higher quality products might be expected to involve higher production costs, not least in terms of the higher costs of the raw materials required (body mix, higher temperature glazes, etc).[24] Some adjustment thus needs to be made for the differences in raw materials and subsequent additional (non-labour) production costs used in the two countries if we are to get closer to the Census concept of value-added. Few of those interviewed within the sample firms visited were able to provide answers to questions about value-added to the NIESR investigators; of those who did reply, many of the answers appeared to the team unrealistically high. Thus we were forced to adopt a more indirect approach: Census estimates of gross value-added to sales were combined with our estimates of turnover per employee to give an 'expected value-added per head' for each of the firms in our sample. Where applicable, this figure was then compared with the self-reported value by the firms. Where the reported value was in line with our expected value (i.e., ± 20%), we left the reported value untouched; where the reported value deviated significantly (i.e., greater than ± 20%), or where no value was reported, we applied the expected value, unless it appeared to the team that there was a plausible reason for the deviation. The resultant weighted average suggests slightly enhanced German advantage, with productivity around 35 higher than in Britain at firm level.

While our calculations are based on employment totals carefully adjusted for part-time working, out-workers, etc, no adjustment has yet been made to the overall totals for differences in average hours worked across the countries. Such adjustment would further increase the aggregate German productivity advantage to around 40 per cent above Britain. While it goes beyond the scope of this inquiry to engage in further such refinements, it seems reasonable to conclude, on the basis of the firm-level data presented above, that a German productivity advantage of around 35-40 per cent above Britain might not be an unreasonable estimate for the tableware sector at present.

In comparison with national statistics, each of our estimates (ie, at plant level, for direct workers only, in terms of value-added per head) clearly suggest a rather greater productivity advantage in Germany's favour. Caution is obviously advisable in light of the small sample sizes in the two countries, but it is perhaps worth recording the most likely reasons for differences between our estimates and those published by each country's statistical authority: Most importantly, our sample focussed exclusively on producers of *tableware,* matched in terms of employment-sizes across the two countries (cf. Table 5). The results at national level, meanwhile, are produced for manufacturers with a somewhat broader range of output (including, for instance, the production of sanitaryware and ceramic tiles), and take no account of differences in size-composition of industries across countries. Also, our employment figures are counted in full-time equivalents, while estimates at national level rely on headcount totals.

4.3. Productivity estimates: Alternative price ratios

As with any comparisons of nominal values across countries, the estimated relative performance of the two countries compared here depends in no small way on the exchange rate used. The years in which this research was conducted (1999-2000) was a time in which the nominal DM/£ exchange rate exhibited considerable volatility – in particular, as the UK participants were keen to point out, a time in which the pound appreciated considerably in relation to the D-Mark. In an effort to avoid distortions to nominal exchange rates caused by say, speculative behaviour in financial markets, economists concerned with cross-country comparisons thus typically employ an alternative exchange factor to convert outputs to common currencies, which takes into account the relative purchasing power of the currencies under consideration. In this section we thus first apply the estimated aggregate purchasing power parity (PPP) exchange rate to our comparative data, and then look at the effects of alternative, sector-specific and quality-adjusted PPP conversion factors. The results are summarised in Table 7.

Official PPP estimates

Our original Table 1 (see p. 4) provides summary data on the relative performance of the household ceramics industries for 1998, and finds little difference in comparative productivity levels *at market exchange rates* of 2.91 DM/£. For that year, the OECD estimate an *aggregate* PPP exchange rate (that is, for total GDP) to be slightly higher, at around 3.04 DM/£ for total GDP. Applying this exchange rate to the original data produced in

Table 1 slightly reduces the German productivity advantage – from 6 to 2 per cent over Britain – in terms of output per head, but makes little difference to the overall conclusion of virtual parity in the relative performance of the two countries at the aggregate level. However, since our comparisons are concerned with the *sectoral* level of tableware-producing plants only, the *aggregate* PPP - estimated for GDP as a whole, and thus including PPPs for *all* goods and services – does not seem to be the most appropriate rate to use in the current context. A more appropriate exchange rate would be that for the sector under consideration – that is, a PPP for tableware only.

Alternative conversion factors

While data are no longer published on the individual (sectoral and product) components for which price-matching is regularly carried out, we are grateful to the UK Office for National Statistics (ONS) for providing access to the unpublished data collected by each country's national statistical agency (in Britain: ONS; in Germany: Statistisches Bundesamt) as part of the international PPP projects of Eurostat and the OECD.[25] The closest available definition for tableware from this source is the individual category of 'tableware and household or toilet articles in porcelain' (Eurostat Basic Heading no. 54010), which collates price observations across the EU for some 28 separate items – for instance, pie-baking moulds, specific forms of plates, cup-and-saucer sets, tableware sets (but, as yet, to our knowledge, *not* to sanitaryware) – made from a wide variety of body pastes *including* earthenware and stoneware. The provisional PPP estimated by Eurostat for this ceramics category for 1999 was 2.62 DM/£ - some 13 per cent below the DM/£ exchange rate estimated for GDP as a whole for that year.[26] Conversion of the *sector-wide* data by this official PPP rate for ceramics suggests a clearer German productivity advantage - of the order of around 17 per cent - over Britain. Comparisons of turnover per employee for the *matched tableware-producing firms* in our sample meanwhile, suggests the German productivity advantage to be closer to 47 per cent on this basis.[27] But further refinements are possible.

The provisional 2.62 DM/£ PPP estimated by Eurostat for tableware as a whole compares well with our own *unweighted* PPP (holding only those observable and quantifiable quality-aspects constant, but unweighted in terms of the quality-mix actually bought by consumers) – of around 2.53 DM/£,

Table 7: The German productivity advantage over Britain: Estimates using alternative conversion factors

		Output per head, UK =100	
	Rate	*Household*	*Matched tableware*
	DM/£	*ceramics sector*	*producing plants*
Conversion factor	1999	(1998[a])	(1999[b])
Market exchange rate	2.92	106	130
GDP PPP	3.01	102	128
Eurostat sectoral PPP			
(unadjusted for quality, unweighted)	2.62	117	147
Unweighted tableware PPP			
(hedonic regression analysis)	2.53	121	152
Quality-adjusted tableware PPP			
(quality-equivalence method)	2.34	131	165

[a] Data for output per head as in Table 1. Exchange rates shown here were adjusted to 1998 levels on the basis of changes in average producer prices. [b] Data for turnover per head as in Table 6.

estimated by way of hedonic regression analysis for a sample of 400 plates (see p. 15 of main text, and Table B4).[28] But both this latter estimate and the Eurostat PPP suffer from the considerable disadvantage (in the context of the present study, at least), in that they fall somewhat short of a full *real* currency equivalent – that is, one which takes full account of differences in the typical quality-mix of products purchased across the countries to produce a *quality-standardised* PPP for conversion purposes. This was attempted in the current study by means of a *quality-equivalence* analysis.

To reiterate on what was done, our sub-sample of 115 plates (62 in the UK, 53 in Germany) was divided, with help from retail buyers, on the basis of their overall mix of physical and aesthetic attributes into four quality-equivalent grades (see earlier pp. 14-17). Price quotations for each plate were then averaged to produce a mean for each quality-grade. These estimates were combined with information on the quantity shares of total sales in each category in the two countries, which were then used as weights in computing the estimated *real* – ie, quality-adjusted - PPP for tableware of 2.34 DM/£, as shown in Table 4.

Using this quality-adjusted PPP to convert estimates of relative productivity to a common currency results in a considerable German advantage - both at sectoral level and in comparing our matched samples of plants: At the *sectoral* level, Germany's productivity advantage now appears substantial

– at around 31 per cent above Britain; within the tightly defined sub-branch of matched *tableware producers*, meanwhile, Germany's real productivity advantage rises to around 65 per cent above the UK.[29]

4.4 The relative quality of UK and German production

Returning to the main focus of the current study, a key result from our matched plant investigations lies in the significantly higher – almost double – average unit value of output estimated for the German plants. Of course, this observed differential may occur simply due to compositional differences in the total output of firms in the two countries – with one country's output containing a greater proportion of say, coffee pots, compared to the other country's apparent specialisation in plates. In an attempt to decompose the higher unit value estimates into 'quality effects' (that is, for a standardised product) versus 'compositional' effects (due to differences in output), we carried out a further analysis, relying once again on our standard dinner plate as a benchmark – this time as an indicator of typical output quality from each of our producers.

Based on what we had seen being produced in the sample plants during our visits (ie, not simply the products which carry the company's backstamp in retail stores), we attempted to mirror the comparisons carried out for the consumer market in Chapter 3. Physical samples of plates typically produced by the manufacturers visited in the two countries were carefully inspected, then ranked on the basis of their combined physical and aesthetic attributes into the same four quality-equivalence grades outlined earlier. In an effort to evaluate the implied *magnitude* of the observed quality differential as valued in the market, we then combined this information with the corresponding average retail prices of plates of *equivalent* qualities. To avoid any potential doubt in the reader's mind, only items *manufactured* in Britain and Germany are compared here.[30] These results of these comparisons are shown in Table 8.

To be quite clear on what is depicted in Table 8, Cols. (1) and (2) show the average retail prices estimated for each of the quality-grades, as estimated in Chapter 3, but only for items *produced* in Britain or Germany.[31] Cols. (3) and (4) show estimated proportions of total domestic output volume – that is, number of pieces, *not* value – produced in each of the quality-grades.

Table 8: Estimated quality-mix of tableware production: Britain and Germany, 1999

	(1)	(2)	(3)	(4)
	Average prices by quality-grade (£) [a]		Quality-mix of domestic production[b]	
Quality grading	UK	D	UK	D
Top	21.31	15.81	15	30
Superior	11.79	8.52	20	30
Standard	8.48	5.63	35	30
Basic	3.17	2.93	<u>30</u>	<u>10</u>
			100	100

Average unit values of domestic production
(weighted by shares of quality grades in UK, Germany)

	UK shares	German shares	Ratio D/UK
At UK prices	9.47	12.79	1.35
At German prices	<u>6.93</u>	<u>9.28</u>	<u>1.34</u>
Quality effect at 'common' prices [c]	8.10	10.90	1.35

[a] German prices converted at 2.971 DM/£, the average market exchange rate for 1999. [b] Distributions are % domestic production volume; all are approximate and have been rounded to the nearest 5 per cent. [c] Geometric average of UK and German prices.

Clearly, a great variety of qualities is produced in both countries. But it seemed to us, from our visits to producers in the two countries, that the *average* quality of the typical piece produced in Germany is noticeably higher than that of the median British manufacture. Based on the opinions of our industry experts, it seems that only around a third of British-produced plates can be categorised to the higher – 'top' and 'superior' – quality grades, compared to around 60 per cent of the German volume. These higher categories, it should be remembered, encompass much of what is produced for the (often very) formal dining market – 'once-in-a-lifetime', and 'wedding list' purchases, often bone china in the UK; the very finest (ie, thinnest) and whitest of the various grades of porcelain produced in Germany - as well as the more design-conscious casual dinnerware, made from those finer grades of earthenware known as 'fine china'. Interestingly, there appears little difference in the proportions of total output of each country produced in the 'standard' grade – ie, that category comprising largely of well-made casualware, perhaps without quite the degree of 'style' or form, or without the fuller range of accessories (eg, serving bowls, platters, or – for the UK, at least – gravy boats) which might otherwise take them – in terms of their physical attributes alone – into a higher classification.

Notably, the greatest disparity in production propensities in the two countries comes about in the differences in the proportions – around a third in the UK, but less than 10 per cent in Germany - of total production classified to the 'basic' quality category.[32] The plates in our sample in this category were almost universally made from cheaper body pastes, with often little chip resistance (in the case of the UK) or of 'greyer' tones. Most were visibly flawed in some way (rough or 'orange peel' surface, firing marks not filed down, etc), poorly decorated (patterns not uniformly applied, colours 'cloudy'), and/or poorly glazed (ie, glaze not uniform or 'bubbled'); many included decorations which were clear imitations of successful designs of their competitors, albeit though instantly recognisable as *not* made by X. Such production tends to be sold through the more price-conscious variety stores and supermarkets in both countries, often as boxed 16- or 20-piece sets, with few, if any, accessories available.

Combining the information on production shares with average prices for each quality grade, we estimate that the average unit value of a typical plate produced in Germany commands a premium of around 35 per cent over the average retail value of a British-made plate. The result is similar, though somewhat less in magnitude, to the results of an earlier inquiry carried out by this Institute into quality differentials in an alternative range of consumer products. That study - based on detailed investigations of quality features, and their corresponding premia in the market place, for women's blouses, secateurs and biscuits - found an average 65 per cent quality advantage for German-made goods over British-made products. The primary research for that study was carried out during the early 1990s, since when considerable 'shake-out' of less productive manufacturers, much new investment and a variety of industrial initiatives have occurred. From a policy perspective, it would of course now seem worthwhile to revisit those original industries to investigate whether the apparent 'improvement' in relative quality performance suggested by the current study – 'only' a 35 per cent German advantage, compared to the earlier 65 per cent estimate - is actually borne out across a range of industries, or whether the ceramic industry is rather doing relatively well in comparison to most of UK manufacturing.

For commentators interested in patterns of international specialisation, of course, even a 35 per cent German quality advantage is of important magnitude. Put another way, the quality differential estimated for our matched items – that is, plate for plate - in Germany more than offsets the lower average output volume (in terms of numbers produced) for that country, and alone accounts for roughly one-third of the observed difference in the average unit values (1.88/1.35) of all tableware items produced in the two countries.

It should be remembered that our sample output - the dinner plate - was chosen to act as a product suitable for relatively easy comparison of quality features across a broad range of manufacturers. The know-how and technology required for the production of flatware, however, differs considerably from the more involved - and costly – production techniques required for the manufacture of more complex and ornate pieces of cast- and hollow-ware (cups, jugs, tea- and coffee-pots, etc). And it does not seem unreasonable to assume that a quality differential for more complex forms of output might be at least as large – perhaps alone explaining as much as two-thirds of the total difference in the average unit values of output. But there may be mitigating effects in terms of the composition of the remaining output - perhaps a greater proportion of flatware in total output in Britain than Germany; a greater diversity of output (ie, a greater range of different products typically manufactured); or a closer correspondence in the mix of output produced to what is required by customers – which themselves have a qualitative element. A much larger and deeper study would be required to consider - and assess - the impact of each of these elements. In the absence of such a study, it seems for now not unreasonable to point to those additional indicators from our case-study investigations which may help shed light on the outstanding (unexplained) portion of the observed differential: One of those factors is the observed higher incidence of flatware in British output totals (65 per cent compared to 52 per cent, based on information from our sample plants), suggestive perhaps of a greater range of more complex production in Germany than in Britain. A further indicator is perhaps the difference in the average batch sizes we estimated for the plants in our sample (around 14,200, on average, for plates at the clayware stage in Britain, compared to just under 9,000 in our German plants), suggesting perhaps a greater degree of fashion-consciousness or faster response time to meeting orders in Germany than in Britain. Both statistics are supportive of the notion that the German quality-advantage is both significant and pervasive.

To avoid misunderstanding, the conclusion reached is not that *all* tableware products manufactured in the UK are of lower quality than those produced in Germany; but rather, that of the great variety of qualities produced in both countries, a higher *proportion* of total output is concentrated in the higher quality-grades in Germany than in Britain. Closer estimates of the absolute magnitude of the quality differential for the full range of tableware output would doubtless be of interest to the industry itself. But from a policy perspective, aside from accepting that differences in average output quality between the countries might be of considerable magnitude, and that clear patterns of quality-specialisation emerge, it seems there is far more is to be gained from seeking to trace the *nature* and *sources* of these productivity and product-quality advantages. In short, there may be important differences in the ways in which production is organised across the two countries which help explain an important part of the differential. We turn now to these additional elements, and deal in turn with differences in physical and human capital across the countries, before seeking to evaluate the impact of these differences on the approaches taken to quality-specialisation within the two countries.

Notes

[20] These figures exclude group employment accounted for by other branches of ceramic manufacturing (eg, sanitaryware, technical ceramics, sales activities) as well as by directly-owned 'overseas' operations, which are these days an important source of additional output.

[21] It is, perhaps, a sad indication of the degree of rationalisation and consolidation in this industry that, during the course of this study, one British manufacturer who originally agreed to participate went into liquidation before the team managed to visit; another two have since called in the receivers; a further two (if news reports in the financial press are to be taken at face value) remain threatened with closure. In Germany, none have closed, but three of our sample firms have since been taken over or sold to new owners.

[22] In fact, a further visit was made in Germany to one of the major specialist producers with a high degree of hand-crafting (*Manufaktur*); however, the degree of manual work involved, both in terms of production and decoration, was deemed too great – and too specialised - for meaningful comparison. This observation was therefore omitted from our study entirely.

[23] That is, excluding the numbers engaged in the manufacture of other ceramic products (eg, tiles, sanitaryware), or in other industries, as well as those who might be deemed employed in the tableware manufacturing sector, but engaged in non-manufacturing activities (eg, retailing operations, factory shops, visitor centres, etc). Sales staff were excluded from all totals. Head office personnel engaged (including say, research and design teams, business managers, etc) were apportioned in relation to the share of manufacturing employment in the sample plants visited.

[24] The high-grade china clay which forms the basis of porcelain, for example, currently sells, on average, for around £200-300 per tonne, depending on the quality. To produce a product which qualifies for classification as bone china, meanwhile, the body paste must contain 50 per cent calcified animal bone, the basic cost of which is currently at least £400 per tonne; meanwhile, the cost of ball clay – the main component for earthenware – is around £100 per tonne. Along with the additional firing costs involved in producing bone china and porcelain, the choice of these two body paste can amount to some 7-10 per cent of total production costs.

[25] Detailed data for individual items, and their product-groups, were previously published – at the beginning of the 1990s – for the then-European Community as *Consumer Prices in the EC* (Eurostat: Luxembourg, 1990 *et seq.).* These publications provided much useful detailed price data for comparative purposes. Given the usefulness of such data for international benchmarking purposes such as these, it can only be hoped that newer volumes will, in time, be published.

[26] The change of year from our earlier comparisons perhaps requires explanation: The PPP project necessitates the collection – and checking - of a range of *average* prices in each participating country for some 5,000 individual items across some 200 or so product-groups ('Basic Headings'), as well as the imputation of prices for non-market goods and services (eg, the public sector). Given the large and ambitious nature of the project, it is not possible for each country to undertake the large number of individual observations necessary on an annual basis; the full range of product-groups is thus subdivided, with new observations for the various products within each Basic Heading collected only every three years. The product-group which best corresponds to our interests in the current paper was 'revisited' in 1999; since these data are likely to correspond more closely to our own observations, carried out in 1999-2000, than those collated in 1996 and simply interpolated (on the basis of general movements in prices in each country for the group as a whole), these are the estimates used here.

[27] Both figures reported ignore differences in annual hours worked across the countries (see fn. 5 above). Such adjustments would, however, raise the German advantage yet further – to around 24 per cent at the sectoral level and to around 52 per cent at the sample firms.

[28] By way of direct comparison, the Eurostat figures for tableware as a whole include *direct* matches between Britain and Germany for a handful of single plates (that is, not part of a larger 'boxed set'), yielding a direct PPP estimate of some 2.65 DM. However, this figure is based on the matched observations only. In aggregating to the Basic Heading level, Eurostat employ a number of 'correction coefficients' to the raw data, including adjustments, for example, for: differences in product prices between capital cities (in which prices are collected) and national averages; inter-temporal differences between the point-in-time observations and annual averages; as well as for missing *direct* observations between any 'pair' of countries by means of *indirect* matches via 'third' countries. (For more on the methodology used by Eurostat, see especially fn. 23 of the earlier paper by Jarvis & Prais, *op. cit.,* 1997.) Issues of confidentiality, and specific assurances to the contrary, prohibit us from revealing further divergences between our own estimate and that of Eurostat.

[29] The estimated PPPs discussed above were used to compute alternative estimates of productivity to those based on nominal exchange rates. However, it is important to consider their validity as a means of converting estimates of production - rather than consumption – to a common currency. The most important factor to take into account when going from consumption to production prices is the possibility of differences in distribution margins in the two countries. Data from the annual retail trade inquiries were used to consider the question of distribution margins but , on balance, our calculations suggest little difference between overall trade margins in the two countries (see Appendix B for details). Finally, we also experimented with calculating production price ratios based only on plates *produced* either in the UK or in Germany. But a major problem of doing this was that for both the hedonic regression and quality-equivalence methods, the smaller sample size led to less robust results. For example, in the hedonic regressions there was little variation in some quality dimensions in the more restricted sample.

[30] Much importing takes place in both Britain and Germany, no longer simply by domestically-based wholesalers and leading retailers, but also - increasingly - by manufacturers themselves. Three distinct strategies are discernible: manufacturers importing the labour-intensive 'components' – eg, decorating, or the more complicated patterns - from lower-cost countries to supplement the plainer, less complex lines easily - and profitably - produced in their highly automated Western European factories; others import the lower value 'blanks' for decoration in the home country, prior to re-packaging and sale; still others supplement the bottom end of their range with imported cheaper lines (perhaps made from lower-grade materials than home-produced units), while continuing to produce the higher-quality (and higher-margin) items domestically. Only articles *known* to have been produced in Britain or Germany – often samples given to us by the companies we visited - were considered for this analysis.

[31] The prices presented are slightly different to those produced in Chapter 3, since our earlier prices included observations for items produced in other – 'third' – countries. This was a better method for the *consumer* market, but is inappropriate for the current analysis of *production.*

[32] Indeed, in gathering our retail prices, we found it rather difficult to locate *German-produced* samples for this quality-grade, since so little of German output is produced in this category. This section of the market, which relies in both countries on largely impulse purchases and is extremely price-sensitive, tends to be limited to sales of 'remainders' from German suppliers; the bulk of sales in this category in Germany being supplied by low-cost imports.

5

Explanations: Physical capital and technology

This Chapter outlines the main differences relating to physical capital within our samples of manufacturing plants, which might be expected to have an effect on productive efficiency. Three aspects are singled out - buildings, kiln technology, and machinery – as of particular importance, on the basis of our discussions with industrialists and factory-level observations in the two countries.

5.1 Buildings

Overall, there was a considerable degree of similarity in the range of buildings in which production activities took place across the countries, with roughly half of the buildings used in each country of single-storey construction, and half multi-storey. The vast majority of the plants in both countries were purpose-built, although – in part, an artefact of history – the average vintage of the German buildings seemed rather less than those of the UK. And we had the impression of a greater spaciousness in the German factories, with more attention paid to the layout and considerably more renovation - removal of walls, enabling the installation of new machinery in the sequence it was used; re-siting of kilns, storage areas, and warehousing, etc – having taken place since the plants were originally built.[33]

In general, multi-storey operations in both counties appeared to be organised along 'line' principles – that is, each floor dedicated to a given production technique (eg, flat- or castware, etc). Where this was not the case, however, we noted a somewhat more systematic - and automatic - approach to the transportation of materials and semi-finishes wares between levels in Germany, through the use of automated conveyor systems (albeit sometimes of a somewhat antiquated nature – for instance, wooden boxed transported by means of overhead pulleys), rather than the typical labourer-pushed trolleys and palettes in Britain.

5.2 Kiln technology

Probably the most important piece of physical capital for any tableware manufacturer is the kiln - or rather, kilns (for there are invariably a variety for the various functions of bisque, glost and post-decoration 'enamel' firing). Major developments over the past decade have led to the introduction of new 'rapid-fire' kilns, capable of carrying out the first ('biscuit') firing in around 5-7 hours - as opposed to the up to 25-30 hours, previously - and reducing decorative firing times to around 30 minutes. In reducing the times wares spend in the kilns so substantially, these rapid firing kilns have three major advantages over the older technology. Firstly, they can be used more flexibly than the older technology, and – by dint of their speed – can cut at least a day from through-put times; secondly, they help reduce production costs through greatly reduced energy requirement - down from around 9-10 per cent of total costs in the firms we visited without them new to around 4-6 per cent in comparable firms with the new technology; and thirdly, there is an important quality effect, in that faster firing times lead to less distortions of ceramic items, and thereby a higher yield. Just under half of the British firms in our sample had invested in new kilns of this type (only two had completely replaced their old stock with the newer technology; many still had a mixture of fast-firing kilns coupled with the older-type – often 'continual fire' push - kilns), compared to three-quarters of the firms in our German sample.[34] All but one of the kilns in both countries were locally sourced.[35]

Fast-firing kilns may be effective in reducing firing times (in one – British – case, from over 48 hours to around 6) and associated energy costs, but many smaller firms in Britain, it seems, in the face of a precarious future, find it difficult to persuade their financiers of the need to invest. Yet companies who had installed this technology reported an additional – to economists - 'external' benefit also. The upheaval involved in the installation often led them to re-think and rationalise the entire firing process. As a result, these companies, for instance, subsequently paid greater attention to loading individual kiln-cars with similar items for optimal firing (fewer distortions due to fewer compromises on temperatures); had taken advantage of the re-engineering simultaneously to install energy-saving ducting equipment, to re-use the air from the kilns for drying purposes; or, had at the same time installed (semi-)automatic loading and unloading technology. Both countries benefited from such reorganisations, but it seemed to us that the benefits were more pervasive in Germany, and often as a result of suggestions by the machinery suppliers. As one British manufacturer with experience of sourcing equipment in both countries put it to us, German machinery suppliers tend to offer their customers a combined *package* of technology, associated advice and know-how; their British counterparts, meanwhile, tend only to supply and install the equipment.

5.3 Production technologies

For an industry typically characterised (by economists, at least) as one of relatively low technology, we were generally surprised at the levels of investment which had clearly taken place in both countries in recent years. The larger companies, in particular, of both countries appeared to have invested heavily in new production technologies, with an impressive arrange of high-pressure casting machinery, isostatic dust presses, direct printers, robotic 'pick-and-place' systems, and the like. One major difference we noted during the course of our factory visits concerns the origin of much of the machinery: virtually all of the newer technology in evidence in the German plants visited was of German origin; the newer technology employed in the British factories, by contrast, was often of more diverse origin – some British, some German, but also French, Italian, and - for robotics, at least – Swiss and Japanese.[36]

Differences were also apparent in the ways in which these high-tech machines were used – and manned - in the two countries. Dust presses, for instance, tended to be set to make only one type of plate at a time in the German plants we visited (so, we were told, as to ensure the optimal granulate mix for the size and form of plate) and were typically manned with one operator responsible for 2-3 machines. In the British firms with this technology, machines were often set to make two differently shaped items – say, a dinner plate and a soup bowl – at the same time (so as to economise on the number of moulds required), usually with one man per machine.

But, from a policy perspective, a distinction needs clearly to be drawn between the requirements of the very large manufacturer in each country, capable of operating at a volume suitable to justify the considerable investments in state-of-the-art technologies - eg, dust-pressers, pressure-casting equipment, and the like - and the needs of the more typical producer, where smaller batches effectively prohibit efficient scales of production.[37] Among smaller companies (say, less than 250 employees) - or those for whom the necessary granulates and 'slips' are not commercially available - investments in such machines may be unsuitable. For these companies, the £250-300,000 required to buy a single dust press is often better spent on (several) automatic or semi-automatic presses, which are less fast, but easier to retool.

Producers of all sizes in both countries were clearly keen to increase their stock of physical capital. Yet it seemed to us that investment decisions were made on a somewhat more informed basis in Germany, where in-house technicians and engineers with a greater knowledge of current technological advances were able better to advise on the relative vintage of equipment on sale, and its suitability for their firm's production. In consequence, most of the new equipment purchased in Germany was fully automatic - eg, fully automatic flatware presses; cup-casting machinery, doing away with the need separately to mould, trim and attach handles to pre-cast 'cups', etc., - and easier to integrate into existing production facilities.

In general, and as with kiln technology, we got the impression of somewhat closer links in Germany than in Britain between the tableware producers and leading machinery manufacturers there (perhaps due to the more consistent reliance on domestic producers for new machinery over the years) - particularly among smaller and medium-sized tableware producers. This leads to a greater degree of collaboration on modifications of standardised equipment and subsequent implementation of more customised technologies.[38] Most importantly, we gained the impression of a marked difference in *approach* to investment between the two countries, with the German firms we visited seeing the machines they purchased as just *part* of a wider package of measures designed with a particular process in mind - for instance, German manufacturers investing in new forming or glazing equipment typically took the opportunity simultaneously to commission their supplier to design and install an associated in-plant transportation system (or, at least, to re-think the existing system) or to use their 'know-how' to use the new equipment most effectively. The British approach, meanwhile, seemed somewhat more piecemeal - with the smaller-scale manufacturers in particular, more likely to buy in standardised 'off-the-peg' machinery, rather than seek out a machinery manufacturer capable of producing the necessary specialist equipment for their needs.[39]

Finally, and undoubtedly in part a response to the higher average labour costs typically faced by the German firms, we noted a markedly greater degree of automation of 'peripheral' activities – eg, sponging, fettling, and particularly, transportation of goods - in the average-sized producer in Germany than in Britain, often as a result of innovations and modifications by the company's in-house maintenance team. Automation of such activities is becoming increasingly common in the UK, but perhaps the potential cost savings are not yet substantial enough to justify the initial outlay.[40]

Notes

[33] Equally, we had the impression of less dust in the air in the German factories (perhaps due better extraction systems in the newer plants there?). While perhaps more noticeable to the lungs of this unaccustomed team than to the professionals working in such factories everyday, one of the British managers we spoke to (with a broad manufacturing background in other sectors) confided to us that this aspect of the industry had been one of the things he had first noticed – and tackled - when taking up his present post. Together with other, similar, relatively simple 'housekeeping' exercises, in so doing the yield rate of the factory had improved from 80 to around 95 per cent – in large part due to the reduction of dust contamination faults during firing.

[34] It may be, of course, that heavier reliance on fast-firing kilns in Germany is in part a reaction to the greater demand for whitewares (as opposed to decorated tableware) in the traditional German markets. The higher relative importance of structural form in whiteware markets has an important consequence for production scheduling, since the customisation of the product begins at the earlier 'forming' stage than for patterned ware, where the decoration is applied post-firing. To some extent, then, British manufacturers face a less urgent need for such newer kilns, since tailoring to customers' needs can be carried out at a later stage - but only at the cost of increased stocks of semi-finished wares. (We discuss this aspect in detail in Chapter 7.)

[35] The only exception was a German-made kiln imported by one of the (larger) British companies in our sample, installed as part of a major reorganisation of its castware lines.

[36] While British decoration equipment was universally acknowledged (by the companies in our sample, at least) as among the best in the world, the UK does not make dust presses. For the rest, according to the very international companies we visited in the two countries, the feeling was expressed that while UK-made machinery and equipment for the ceramics industry has improved considerably in recent years - and while many of the major new ideas for machine design originate in Britain - the greater durability *and reliability* of German engineering means that Germany remains more successful in manufacturing - and exporting - this equipment.

[37] For a dust-presser to be economically reset with new moulds, we were told, minimum batch sizes of 10,-15,000 – equivalent to some 1½-2 weeks' single-shift production - are typically required. On direct printing decoration machines, the retooling costs might only be justified on the basis of 3-4 days' worth of plates of identical size and colour.

[38] Among the larger firms of both countries, where R&D activities are often carried out in-house, we got the impression of a more 'ambitious' nature of R&D activity among the German manufacturers than was typical in Britain, with the former less content than the UK firms we visited to wait until technology was available, but rather to help develop new technology *with specific manufacturing needs in mind*. In Britain, it seems that except for the very largest firms, the development of equipment is perceived as an activity outside the domain of the tableware industry itself; it is left to the suppliers to innovate. Neither strategy is necessarily better; but by working together with the manufacturers, it seems German firms get faster access to the latest technology.

[39] The point is perhaps best illustrated by one of our observations: Company 'X' is a medium-sized British earthenware

manufacturer. In touring the production facilities, considerable investment in new technology was readily apparent. The company had recently invested considerable sums in two (foreign-made) pressure-casting machines - equipment usually seen by the team in only the very largest UK factories we had visited. The investment - both in monetary and reorganisational terms - had been substantial; but since these machines had been developed more with porcelain production in mind, rather than the larger-particle earthenware mixture typically used by the company, the firm had been forced to add more water to the slip than anticipated and a major benefit of pressure-casting – ie, lower drying costs – had been lost!

[40] As one impressive British manufacturer calculated, it would be hard to justify the replacement of replacing two labourers each costing the company £15,000 per year to transport wares around the factory, with an automated transport system which would require some £750,000 to install – an estimated payback time of around 25 years. This equation may not be quite so straightforward however, since it omits personnel costs involved in 'tracking down' missing items due to misplacement – and the dusting costs for items 'found' long after they set off!

6

Explanations: Human capital

A key aim of this inquiry was to investigate – and seek to delineate - those aspects of workforce skills which contribute particularly to productivity and high quality production. From an economist's perspective, we need to consider whether the ways in which labour is – as we shall show, somewhat differently – deployed in the two countries adequately reflects differences in the relative costs and availability of that labour. From a policy perspective, the question becomes whether the different mixes of quantity *and quality* of labour currently observable are sufficient for long-term survival. This Chapter examines in detail the principal differences in skills, manning levels and working methods in the two countries. We first look briefly at the major differences in formal qualification levels of shopfloor employees in the two countries. We then examine cross-country differences in the deployment and skill requirements of labour in five areas of activity: production workers; technical support; supervisory personnel; the design function; and research and development.

6.1 Qualifications of shopfloor workers

The mature nature of the tableware industry ensures a high degree of specialisation of labour in both countries, in which many of the shopfloor operations are largely routine and require limited knowledge of other production activities. Since few of shopfloor positions require a long formal training prior to commencement, few employers in either country set any great store on the need to recruit formally qualified personnel for most production-line activities.[41] In consequence, only a minority of shopfloor workers in either country held vocational qualifications at the main 'craft' level – certified in Germany through the award of the *Berufsabschluss* (usually at the end of a 3- to 3½ year apprenticeship) and, in Britain, at National Vocational Qualification (NVQ) Level 3 – although the proportions vary considerably across the countries. Some 15 per cent of shopfloor workers held craft-level qualifications in production-relevant subjects in our German sample plants, compared with just under 5 per cent in the British plants we visited (see Table 9). The significance of this ratio is perhaps easier to understand when put conversely: approximately one in every 7 shopfloor workers in Germany held formal vocational qualifications, compared to roughly 1 in 22 in the British plants we visited. In both countries, these qualified personnel tended to be heavily concentrated in what might be termed as technical support functions, such as machine maintenance and mould-making, or employed as production supervisors and foremen. Of those

Table 9: Employment distribution and skill propensities in typical British and German tableware producing plants [a]

	UK		Germany	
	% total employment	% craft-qualified [b]	% total employment	% craft-qualified [b]
Management/admin [c]	8.7	n/a	13.7	n/a
Shopfloor workers [d]	91.3	4.6	86.3	15.2
Of whom (by activity):-				
supervisors/foremen	5.5	20.0	5.0	50.0
Production activities				
- Direct production [e]	61.2	0.0	56.4	7.0
- Warehousing, packaging and dispatch	10.0 f[e]	..	13.8	..
- Peripheral activities	10.2	..	6.2	..
Technical support activities				
- Maintenance	2.6	84.0	3.3	90.0
- Mould-makers	2.3	23.9	2.0	100.0
	100.0		100.0	
Typical numbers employed	438.0		413.0	

[a] Unweighted averages across the firms of our sample. For purposes of comparability, the numbers engaged in clay-mixing and slip-making activities have been excluded from the totals for each company. [b] Qualified with at least NVQ-level 3 in Britain; *Berufsabschluss* in Germany. [c] Figures exclude sales personnel; include general factory management and administration, imputed proportions of head office personnel, design and R&D functions, etc. [d] Includes all shopfloor workers customarily described as 'direct workers', ie, those involved in all aspects of the production of the firm's output – from the forming, glazing, etc operations to those in warehousing, compilation of orders, product-chasing, etc. [e] Includes making and forming operations, decorating, glazing and firing. [f] British figure includes estimate for one firm where these activities were contracted out. Figures may not sum to 100 due to rounding to nearest decimal place. n/a – not available... – less than 0.5 per cent.

employed in the numerically important category of product-making activities, few of those in either country involved in production activities held formal craft qualifications: in fact, just 7 per cent in Germany; none at all in Britain, since qualifications for ceramics manufacture do not exist at this level.[42]

6.2 Production workers: Differences in deployment

The optimal mix of skills in every factory depends heavily on the production mix (high-quality dinnerware; everydayware; flat v. hollow-ware; white- v. decorated ware, etc) and the size of operation. Each manufacturer has his own nomenclature for the various tasks around his factory, but several numerically important areas can be defined across all the companies in our study, as follows: 'making' – combining the activities of forming and casting operations, cleaning the formed wares ('trimming and fettling'); glazing operations; decorating; machine maintenance; and mould-making. We illustrate our main observations regarding differences in the deployment of personnel by taking a brief 'virtual tour' around each of the various departments in turn.

6.2.1 Making operations
Given the differences in the technologies adopted by the plants in our study, there was inevitably considerable variation in the organisation of 'forming' activities. We outlined above the typical differences in the manning levels for highly sophisticated dust presses (cf. p. 33); but there were also considerable differences between the countries among smaller operations with less advanced technologies at their disposal. It seemed to us that in making activities, the average German operative was typically expected to be responsible simultaneously for several (two *or more*) machines, compared to just one (or, *at maximum*, two) in Britain, and was often expected to complete a somewhat wider range of tasks than his British counterpart, typically including the peripheral activities also. By way of illustration, we take the widespread example of semi-automatic cup production.

In the average British factory, the following sequence is not uncommon: One operative feeds 1-2 semi-automatic jollying machines with clay. The jollied 'cups' go down the line, where three handle-fixers apply slip and attach the handles. Two operatives then sponge off the excess slip before loading them onto the dryer. After drying, three fettlers grind off the rough edges, before a further person carries out quality control. The mugs are then transported - by a labourer - around the factory, and then loaded onto kiln furniture by another operative ready for biscuit firing. The labour input to this stage alone amounts to some 10½ full-time equivalents (excluding the labourer), plus the associated labour of one handle-caster and one 'deseamer' – that is, a full team of 12½. These dozen or so workers together produce around 6,000 cups per day.

In the average German factory, the team more typically comprises some 8½ full-time equivalents:- one loading 2-3 machines with clay, one caster-cum-deseamer, four in handle attachment (1 loads the cups into the machine; 1 inserts the handles and attaches; 2 wipe off excess slip and load the cups directly onto the drying machine). Post-drying, three fettlers (2 scrapers, 1 sponger) grind the cups and load them directly onto kiln furniture, before the mugs are taken for firing. No separate quality controller is required; that job is done by the fettlers. The cups will typically be transported automatically to the kiln, but that need not concern us here, since we did not include the labourer in the British example. This team also produces 6,000 cups per day.

This *combination* of tasks was a pervasive feature of the German plants we visited. Indeed, one of the striking differences visible to each member of the team following visits to similar plants in the two countries was of the many more workers typically employed around the British plants who appeared to be unattached to specific departments or lines, but who nevertheless contribute to the definitions of production workers in both countries. Many of these were involved in quality control-type activities – known variously as inspectors, selectors, sorters, and checkers, etc; as many again were involved in less specific tasks – often little more than moving goods from one area of the factory to another (or checking on their whereabouts!) – with titles such as labourers, placers, kiln-emptiers, wipers out, floaters, progress chasers, and the like. These two peripheral groups together accounted for some 10 per cent of total factory employees in the UK plants in our sample – roughly 1 in every 10 factory workers. Quality control personnel were far fewer in Germany – selection tasks often being combined with other activities there. And many of the transportation jobs had been automated out of the system.

In consequence, far fewer workers in the German plants could be classified to this 'peripheral' category – equivalent to around 1 in every 16 workers.[43]

6.2.2 Glazing operations

Automatic glazing equipment is now widely available and relatively cheap, so we were somewhat surprised at the incidence of manual glazing seen in both countries; but it seems that for small batches or oddly-shaped items, hand-dipping is a widely-preferred method.[44] Average dipping speeds seem considerably lower in Germany than Britain, at around 1,800-2,000 items per person per shift, compared to around 3,000 per person in the UK; but due to the larger batch sizes typically processed in the UK plants, the British teams tend to be involved in dipping many more of the *same* items (for instance, a large batch of cups or mugs) for the entire shift, while the German glazers handle a wider variety – usually a minimum of 10-12 – of different items in each shift.

6.2.3 Decorating

By far the most labour-intensive aspect in tableware production comes at the decoration stage. The standard method of decoration throughout the industry remains the manual application of lithographed transfers ('decals') to glost-fired whitewares by large numbers of semi-skilled operatives. Few come with any formal decoration qualifications in either country; most learn on the job.[45] Although largely unskilled, it may take many months for operatives to reach efficient performance levels - around six months, according to manufacturers in both countries, for the simpler patterns; several years to become fully efficient at applying more complex decorations to hollowware. Holding on to good decorators is thus seen as an important aspect of business strategy, and manufacturers have responded in both countries by offering increasingly flexible working arrangements – flexible hours, shorter working days, time off during school holidays, etc - in order to encourage their best workers to stay. But this is not always easy to fit in with production schedules. Thus, manufacturers in both countries look to reduce the labour content – and, equally importantly, labour costs - of decorating through a range of approaches.

For simpler shapes, a variety of levels of automation are available: for flatware, for instance, direct printing equipment can be used to print up to eight colours at a time (the illusion of even more, if the engraved plates can be carefully aligned); heat release machines can be used to apply transfers to flat-sided mugs and cups; simple 'stripe' and 'banded' designs can be fairly easily automated for most wares through the use of jigs and rollers. But for many of the items which make up the standard dinner service (for instance, jugs, gravy boats, etc), automation of the decoration function is less feasible, due to the often curved and asymmetric nature of the items involved.

Faced with higher wage costs, the response of many German firms is to seek, where possible, to 'outsource' the less urgent (and usually simpler) decorating activities to the specialist decorating units (often conveniently located close to the German borders) of the Czech Republic and Poland. The practice is relatively widespread in Germany, and accounts for the equivalent of roughly 20 per cent of total output volume. Quality is typically maintained through supervision of the off-site work by the German manufacturer's own foremen. The net saving in labour costs – that is, net of supervisory personnel, transport costs and breakages in transit – amounts to roughly 30 per cent in comparison to German decorators.[46]

Greater savings still – around 50 per cent less in comparison to the costs of manual decorating in Germany - can be achieved through the use of direct printing technology, but for the reasons set out above (small batches, three-dimensional objects), they are often less appropriate for the task in hand than the flexibility afforded by manual operatives.[47] Such machines appeared to us rather more common in the UK than in Germany for the processing of flatware – probably as a result of the larger average batches typically decorated in the UK, and the somewhat higher proportion of flatware in total output volume. For the more complicated forms, however, the lower average wage costs typically faced by the British manufacturer make the incentive to find an alternative source of labour, as yet, less pressing.

6.3 Technical support

In addition to the direct production workers of the shopfloor, two relatively skilled departments – machine maintenance and mould-cutting - are common throughout the industries of both countries, regardless of the size of operation.

6.3.1 Machine maintenance

Since decreasing batch sizes require an ever higher incidence of resetting and retooling of machinery, few companies in either country are prepared do without the constant on-site presence of an in-house maintenance crew. Only one of the companies in our sample had been prepared to 'contract out' completely the maintenance operations; others buy in engineering services for routine and/or emergency maintenance, or for substantial overhauling of major equipment (kilns, spraying machines, etc), but keep qualified on-site crews for the frequent retooling and resetting machines. Despite the small absolute numbers involved in relation to total employment, we noted a significant difference in the relative size of the typical maintenance crews in the two countries, with the German crews proportionately larger than in Britain. Expressed in terms of the numbers of maintenance personnel to the numbers employed in production activities, the German crews were roughly a third larger than the British maintenance teams, equivalent to roughly 1:23 production workers in Germany, 1:31 in Britain. The higher numbers of maintenance personnel in Germany are doubtless in large part a direct result of the more frequent retooling of machines typically required for the smaller batches processed there; and we got the impression of a greater degree of routine maintenance and modification of standardised technology in the German plants.

Maintenance is a highly-skilled area. There was, in consequence, within the crews, little difference in the average proportions of maintenance teams with formal craft qualifications in the two countries, but a greater tendency for those employed in such activities in Germany to be qualified as electrical engineers, rather than as mechanical engineers or with more general craft qualifications (for instance, as toolmakers, joiners, etc), as was more typical in the UK.

With production technologies becoming ever more sophisticated, manufacturers in both countries felt that engineering skills would become increasingly important in the future, yet only the half of German factories seemed willing themselves to train for future requirements– with roughly one apprentice for every 7 employed in maintenance. These firms tended to be the larger-scale operations, and with a greater proportion of high-tech equipment. None of our British sample plants had any apprentices in these areas at the time of our visit.

6.3.2 *Mould-makers*

Perhaps the most difficult-to-replace personnel at shop-floor level are the mould-makers – comparable, in branches of metal manufacturing, to the highly-skilled tool-cutters - required for the continual replacement of the gypsum moulds used by pressing and casting equipment. The moulds must typically be replaced after every 50-60 impressions – perhaps twice as often if a particularly delicate relief pattern is involved.[48] In consequence, mould-makers are particularly important for manufacturers relying heavily on older-type automatic and semi-automatic pressing machinery, and those with a high proportion of slip-casting in their product mix.

Mould-makers are thus highly sought after in both countries – and, we were told, increasing 'hard to come by'. Though previously often a job handed down from father to son, these days the general contraction in the ceramics industries has made it difficult to attract new recruits for this highly-skilled occupation in both countries.

Virtually all of the chief mould-makers in our sample firms in both countries were formally qualified in the task. But there was a considerable difference in the 'teams' under them: all of the German teams were formally qualified in mould-cutting, compared to just one in five in the British plants in our sample. Given the clearly higher relative importance attached to structural form in Germany, it seemed to us astonishing that none of the companies in our sample seemed to be taking steps to train for their future requirements.

6.4 Supervisory personnel

The importance attached to the qualified foreman in Germany has been well-documented in previous analyses by this Institute.[49] Yet while the differences in both the numbers employed *and* in the numbers formally qualified are perhaps less divergent in this industry than those noted in previous studies of other sectors, the importance of the difference in the proportions formally qualified – a half of all German foremen holding at least the

Berufsabschluß, compared to roughly 1 in 5 of the British supervisory personnel - should not be overlooked. In common with those earlier studies (of a decade and more ago), this investigation also found evidence of a somewhat broader *range* of responsibilities typically undertaken by the German supervisors. In brief, it seemed to us that much more delegation of responsibility was involved, with the German foremen themselves carrying out the weekly production planning required to meet output objectives; expected alone to ensure that the machinery of their 'lines' be properly and routinely maintained; in quickly recognising and reporting back the sources of any problems in production; and in suggesting new machinery that might be more appropriate for the task in hand. While all of this may sound unexceptional to the informed reader, perhaps the major point of departure between the German foreman and his British counterpart lies in the timescale: the smaller batches typically produced in Germany, and the seemingly greater structural diversity of total production volume, effectively requires that the foreman both foresees and puts in place the necessary solutions to any potential delays to processing *before* production begins.

6.5 Design teams

The importance of good design was consistently reported as of ever-greater significance in building (and maintaining) a competitive edge by all case-study respondents in both countries.[50] Adding value by means of aesthetic enhancement - new surface patterns, new shapes and forms (eg, salad bowls, underplates, etc) - was thus seen as a major objective by all our the firms in our study. A variety of approaches is used - from in-house design teams to working to customer-specified designs (provided directly by the larger retail chains and corporate customers), to the wholesale 'buying in' of designs and the use of freelance designers. In practice, most firms use some combination of all of these strategies, although there is greater reliance on in-house development in Germany (accounting for around three-quarters of new designs marketed in Germany, compared to just under 60 per cent of new designs in Britain); input from freelance designers in Germany tends to be limited to a handful of 'known designers', well-acquainted with the company's design profile and production capabilities. British manufacturers, by contrast, argue that outsiders and freelancers help to strengthen the design portfolio of the company by bringing in fresh ideas; yet, of the almost 20 per cent of 'fresh ideas' bought in by our British sample, one-third of these were bought directly from the decal manufacturers supplying the lithographs used to apply decoration to tableware. To the average German manufacturer, there seems little point in buying in ideas if these are not on an *exclusive* basis.[51]

Few firms in either country were prepared to forego completely the perceived benefits of a distinct – often 'stand alone', or combined 'design and marketing' – in-house design department.[52] Of course, the numbers employed are not large in either country, averaging around one per cent of total employment in the firms in our sample.[53] And – as might be expected in an industry of such varying degrees of design-consciousness - there was no clear (monotonic) relationship between firm size and the size of their design departments; the only clear result in this respect was that, where a department existed, no firm appeared to see any merit in appointing a sole designer working in isolation.

Though, perhaps in this field more than any other in the trade, paper qualifications are by no means an adequate measure of a designer's say, capacity in the field, virtually all of those employed in design activities across our sample firms - 90 per cent in the UK; 99 per cent in Germany - held some form of vocationally relevant qualification. In some ways, we might say that the British designers were rather better qualified than their German counterparts, holding at least *graduate*-level qualifications (NVQ Level 4), following the completion of a full-time 3-year degree or HND course;[54] the members of the German design teams, meanwhile, were more likely to be qualified at the lower *craft* level (equivalent, in NVQ terms, to Level 3), following the completion of a part-time industrial apprenticeship. And there was a further distinction concerning the nature of the qualifications held in the two countries: In the British teams, just over half of those working as designers had qualified from, what might be described as, *artistic* courses (often, for instance, from fine arts degrees or with qualifications in graphics design), compared to only 40 per cent in our German sample. The typical German artistic qualification was more likely to be a university degree in *industrial* design, or a craft-level apprenticeship as an industrial decorator (*Dekormaler, Kerammaler*). By contrast, just a third of the British designers held what we call here, *faute de mieux,* technical qualifications - that is, including some theoretical instruction in the properties of, for instance, ceramic colours, constraints to form, or glazing techniques, etc – compared to 57 per cent of the German teams.[55]

Undoubtedly, artistic flair is an important element of a designer's 'toolbag'. And artistic skills may play a more significant role in the British design process than in Germany, because of the greater relative importance of surface design (decoration) over structural form in Britain. Yet it is perhaps also worth noting the comments we heard repeatedly from a number of representatives of large retail chains in the UK with experience of sourcing (often own-brand) goods from UK tableware suppliers: for instance, development times too long (up to 12 months) between commissioning new designs and getting the product made, as design briefs go back and forth between retailer and manufacturer; colours 'not quite right' for the increasingly popular 'mix-and-match' ranges; or colours not as anticipated once produced. While all agreed that British paper-based designs were among the best in the world, as one buyer put it, 'what you see on the concept board is not necessarily what you get'.

This, of course, is not to say that the German design teams get it right every time; but it seems that the greater technical understanding of the German designers does ensure that they have a clearer idea from the outset as to what can be realistically (re-)produced – for instance, how close they might get to an on-paper colour, once that colour is translated into ceramic pigment and glazed; and which decoration technique – decals or thermal printing - might be best used to ensure the desired result.

While colour is an important consideration in the trend-setting market, sales of (undecorated) whiteware are becoming increasingly popular in both markets – particularly at the upper end, we were told, as it is more likely to endure the changing tastes (for redecoration) than coloured or patterned designs.[56] As sales of whitewares increase, structural form plays an increasingly important role in differentiating between manufacturers' output. But to be viably produced, new forms need to be designed with a knowledge of the constraints and structural properties of ceramics when subjected to the kiln. (Poor design can cost dearly if too many pieces distort during firing.) Here it seems that the role of the skilled *Kerammodelleur* - qualified as a result of a three-year industrial apprenticeship, and responsible largely for the modelling of 3-dimensional prototypes of new designs - goes a long way to 'streamlining' the range of goods to be economically produced in Germany than is typically the case in the UK.

These skills exist – to an extent - in Britain, according to manufacturers with experience of graduates from one highly specialised course in 'Ceramics Design' in the UK. But they exist at a higher level of *post-graduate* qualification, following at least 5 years' full-time post-secondary *university education* in the UK. 'Industrial' experience is limited to work placements spent entirely in company design departments - *not* on the shopfloor. The numbers qualifying amount to barely a dozen each year. Many go on to work as freelance designers, not as part of a product development team within firms.

In Germany, meanwhile, the predominant route to these skills remains the company-based practical training via the apprenticeship system, including block instruction in the theoretical aspects of ceramic design and production at the vocational colleges.[57] The numbers qualifying in Germany are also not large – around 100 a year – but are sufficient for the manufacturers there to use *in combination with* more aesthetic design skills to be able to launch and produce cost-effectively some 2-3 new structural forms each year. In form design, a technical background is undoubtedly important. But it is likely to be the greater degree of *shopfloor* experience that gives the German designer his enhanced appreciation of the various degrees of difficulty involved in different production techniques. And his greater knowledge of in-house production technologies, makes it easier for him to capitalise in his designs on the particular strengths of *his* company. In Britain, it seems that the designer is not expected to consider these aspects. His task is to come up with an attractive design. Considerations as to *how* best to produce those designs are typically left as an issue for the production department.

Given the repeated importance attached to design in the tableware industry (we might say, manufacturing generally), it seems remarkable how little attention has so far been paid - by producers, researchers, and policy-makers alike - to trying to understand the optimal mix of skills required for successful product development. For this industry at least, there seems a marked distinction in what is required from design teams across the countries.

6.6 Research & development teams

All firms innovate to some degree. But, unlike design, the desire to engage in research and development (R&D) activity was a somewhat secondary consideration in many of the firms in our sample. Thus only around half of our firms in both countries had separate R&D departments. Unsurprisingly perhaps, those firms which had them tended to be either very large firms (those with say, more than 700 employees), or those with specialist technical needs (most importantly, those producing a high proportion of hotelware).[58] The other half in both countries were content to carry out any necessary R&D activities using in-house technical and engineering personnel - often maintenance and laboratory testing crews - as required. Several of the German firms in this category reported working closely with equipment suppliers to adapt machinery for their needs. Collaboration with outside agencies (university departments, specialist research institutes) was generally deemed unnecessary for these smaller companies in both countries.

Even in those firms with separate R&D departments, the total numbers engaged on such activities were, unsurprisingly, small; and there was little difference between the countries in the numbers engaged - at roughly 0.6 % - in relation to total employment. Only four of the firms in each of the countries visited provided adequate data on the skills and qualifications of their R&D workers for analysis; these firms tended to be considerably larger in Germany than in Britain, so the figures that follow must be interpreted with utmost caution, as the small sample sizes make for potentially great misinterpretation.[59]

Caveats aside, from our (sub-)samples of firms, while all of those employed in both countries held a relevant technical qualification, a slightly greater proportion of total R&D staff held advanced qualifications (at technician level or above) in the UK than in Germany – some 80 per cent in Germany, compared to all in our British samples.[60] That said, there appeared to be little difference in the numbers trained to graduate level in Britain and Germany (at 76 and 71 per cent, respectively). The main point of departure seemed to be a rather greater emphasis on ceramics engineering qualifications in the UK (accounting for four-fifths of the total), compared to a more equal distribution between ceramics and more general engineering degrees in Germany.

We repeat, the numbers are small and these statistics should be viewed with caution. Yet it is perhaps worth noting our impressions of the differences in the nature of R&D activities typically undertaken in the two countries.

Based on our discussions with *all* of the sample firms with separate R&D departments in both countries, we had the impression of a clear emphasis in the UK on ceramics development - in particular, into the technical properties of new body pastes, as well as much research work into the removal of lead from glazes and colours. While product development is not a low priority in Germany, it seems that proportionately more research activity is devoted to process engineering considerations – for instance, seeking to adapt production techniques from other industries (eg, injection moulding) to ceramics manufacture, improving glazing technology, etc.

Notes

[41] The reader should note that our definition of shopfloor workers differs somewhat to that typically used by industry. Where the usual distinction tends to be made between shopfloor workers or management according to whether employees are hourly-paid (direct production workers, warehousing and dispatch employees, etc) or salaried (usually including supervisory and maintenance personnel, and often mould-cutters). For the purposes of our analysis, it seems more fitting to divide between the habitual place of work of employees. Thus our totals for management and administration have been reduced to allow a separate tabulation of qualification levels for supervisors, maintenance personnel and the like within the 'shopfloor' category. Our definition of *industry-relevant* qualifications includes qualifications in ceramics specialties, as well as the more general industry-wide qualifications, such as electrician, mechanic, etc. Workers qualified in non-industrial occupations – for instance, in clerical work, or as retail assistants, etc – were excluded from our totals of qualified workers in both countries.

[42] Neither country appears to train large numbers to formal vocational levels for ceramics occupations. Just 211 gained their craft-level vocational certificate (*Berufsabschluß*) in ceramics in 1999, just over half of whom qualified with the generalist *Keramiker* qualification (*Source*: Statistisches Bundesamt, *Bildung und Kultur Fachserie 11, Reihe 3, Berufliche Bildung 1999*, pp. 131, 140. Figures. refer to those qualifying in occ. nos. 1210 *Keramiker*, 1211 *Industriekeramiker*, 1212 *Kerammodelleur*, 5140 *Glas- u. Kerammaler*.) While, in the same year, some 268 UK candidates gained 'skill-based' qualifications in ceramics occupations at the lower NVQ-Level 2, these qualifications tend to be rather narrower in scope than those typically offered in Germany. Candidates are awarded a certificate on the basis of their competence in one of a narrowly-defined function (for instance, 'processing raw materials' *or* 'forming ceramic items' *or* 'firing ceramic items'), for which the employer receives a subsidy for each newly-qualified employee under the auspices of the various government training schemes. Unlike the requirements for the award of the German *Berufsabschluß*, British candidates are not expected to rotate around departments: the idea is rather to certificate the skills they typically use in their current jobs; NVQs at Level 3 - comparable to the lowest level deemed worthy of certification in Germany - do not exist in Britain for production workers in this industry. (We are grateful to Dominic Manley of the City and Guilds of London Institute for these data.) For the sake of completeness, some 8 per cent of the British shopfloor workers held NVQ Level 2 qualifications.

[43] Totals for peripheral activities do not include those assigned to warehousing and dispatch activities.

[44] This did not, however, satisfactorily explain its use to the exclusion of automatic dipping in around half of the factories in our sample. The full answer, it seems, has rather more to with the quality – ie, coverage - advantages afforded by greater flexibility from hand- as opposed to automatic-dippers for awkwardly-shaped articles in Germany; in the UK, often more to do with the potential cost of installing glaze-recovery systems.

[45] There is an interesting distinction between the two former Republics of what is now the German Federal Republic in this aspect: while craft-level vocational qualifications specific to ceramic decoration (*Kerammaler*) do exist for the former West Germany, they tend to be taken only by those who wish to specialise later in surface *design*, or by those hoping to

work as specialist painters of high value ornamental ware. The greater number of specialist qualifications for the ceramics sector in the former East of the country in part reflects the pre-*Wende* importance of this sector as a major source of foreign revenue. In consequence, many of those employed in the (one) former-East German plant we visited reported craft qualifications as 'skilled decorators' (*Dekorfacharbeiter*).

[46] One of the most significant distinctions we noted between the two countries' production strategies related to the use and location of that part of manufacturing carried out outside the physical limits of the companies themselves. While in both countries, many of the very large operations make use of external manufacturers far away to supplement their domestically produced ranges, equally important considerations for the industry as a whole – and for those concerned with industrial policy – concern the differences in the ways in which total domestic output is shared among domestic producers. We were struck in our factory visits in Germany by the high degree of *Zulieferung* (lit: subcontracting) taking place there, whereby lesser-known producers contract to supply the better-known manufacturers with *finished* items (often including the 'brand' back-stamping and packaging). This 'internal trade' has the advantage that the brand-owner can still stamp this output as 'Made in Germany' and thus maintain the 'quality hallmark' in the consumer's mind. In other firms, German-made semi-finished whitewares are sent for decoration to nearby Poland and the Czech Republic, but re-imported back into Germany for the final glazing and packaging operations. Substantial 'outward processing' of full ranges beyond the German borders, it seems, is reserved merely for those very long runs of standard-ware used to supplement higher-grade domestic ranges. The British approach to outsourcing meanwhile, appeared to us quite different, with UK firms adopting one of two distinct approaches: Most were content to buy in low-cost 'blanks' from competitor companies for decoration and dispatch. Among the very largest companies, however – and, despite considerable investment in new technology over recent years – an increasingly proportion of total output is composed of bought-in finished wares from lower-cost overseas producers, often simply to be repackaged (and perhaps back-stamped) for sale alongside – in quality terms - a 'virtually indistinguishable' range of domestically-produced items. A considerable profit is, it seems, still from the provision of the original design. (The quote is from a representative of one of the companies with a long experience of doing so. The result, meanwhile, mirrors that found in a recent comparison of medical equipment manufacturers in the same countries by our colleagues, R Anderton and S Schultz, *Explaining Export Success in the UK and Germany: A Case Study of the Medical Equipment Industry*, London: Anglo-German Foundation, 1999.) For a fuller account of the extent and forms of external processing arrangements, together with a summary of relative prices for quality-matched goods produced by a range of foreign suppliers, see *Outsourcing, Outward Processing and Output Quality*, by V Jarvis and M O'Mahony, NIESR, 2002.

[47] Even for flatware, many manufacturers in both countries still prefer the traditional labour-intensive application of 'decals' over more high-tech methods – supposedly, for reasons of greater refinement (better colours and higher resolution) possible with the decoration by transfer. (Undoubtedly also due to batch sizes too small to warrant the £1,000+ per colour for each engraving plate for direct printing machines - and the considerable costs and time involved in re-tooling.)

[48] The moulds for the more advanced equipment – eg, high pressure casting, dust pressing – typically last for thousands of impressions, but are unsuitable for all but granulate pressing, since the gypsum helps in the drying process. These moulds tend to be produced by specialist external manufacturers – often the machinery suppliers themselves.

[49] See, for instance, A Daly *et al.*, Productivity, Machinery and Skills in a sample of British and German manufacturing plants, *National Institute Economic Review* (February 1985); H Steedman and K Wagner, A Second Look at Productivity, Machinery and Skills, *Ibid.* (November 1987); and specifically, SJ Prais and K Wagner, Productivity and Management: the Training of Foremen in Britian and Germany, *Ibid.* (February 1988).

[50] The importance of good design for economic success, and the British lack of attention to either the issue or practice, has been repeatedly emphasised in previous analyses for the sector. See, for instance: the section on 'Priorities for Action' in the joint British Ceramic Confederation-Department of Trade and Industry *Tableware Strategy Group: Second Report* (November 1996); or the more recent *Strategic Analysis of the Ceramics Industry in Staffordshire* by ECOTEC Research & Consulting, jointly commissioned by the City of Stoke-on-Trent, Staffordshire Training & Enterprise Council, the British Ceramic Confederation and the Government Office for the West Midlands, (March 1999), esp. pp. 41-2.

[51] This reliance by the smaller manufacturers in the UK on the decal manufacturers to supply designs, and concerns as to the efficacy of this approach, are of long-standing: In his study of design carried out in the 1930s, (German-born) Nikolaus Pevsner notes the 'established fact that 90 per cent of the firms [in Stoke-on-Trent] have no proper designer…The decoration manager […] may have attended evening classes in an art school, or he may not. Sales experience is regarded as more important than a grasp of design. So far as design is concerned, his work consists of the buying of lithographs for transfer, the adapting of hackneyed old patterns, and the imitation of new ones from next door.' *An Enquiry into Industrial Art in England* (CUP, 1937), p. 79.

[52] In smaller companies, without a separate design department, the managing director often takes on the role. Only one of our German companies was willing to forego an in-house design department completely, preferring instead to buy in or

licence designs (but *only* on an exclusive basis) from freelancers; and just two in our British sample.

[53] Design functions are very rarely carried out at 'plant' level; the vast majority form part of the central functions of the company's 'Head Office'. It thus makes little sense to refer to the design department for a given plant, since the discoveries and strategies are typically made available to the company as a whole. In expressing the numbers employed as a proportion of total employment, therefore, we use in this section total company employment as our 'denominator'. This adjustment, however, has no bearing on the productivity results reported in Chapter 4. There an imputed ratio of total head office personnel was applied to each of the plants in our sample in proportion to the sample plant's share of total manufacturing employment.

[54] Indeed, many had qualified at the higher NVQ Level 5-equivalent, from post-graduate (MA) courses in ceramics design (see text).

[55] As with any classification, there is some difficulty in categorising certain qualifications, due to a heavy overlap in the content of both categories. Qualifications in 'Ceramics Design' are here classified to the category of technical qualifications, due to the inclusion of instruction in the technical properties of ceramics.

[56] Quite why consumers are willing to change even their sofas more often than their tableware remains one of the enduring questions – here unanswered also – among British manufacturers.

[57] *Berufsschulen*; equivalent to British colleges of further – *not* higher – education.

[58] For the reasons outlined in footnote 53 it makes little sense to refer in this discussion to plant-level activities. Our results here are therefore presented in relation to total firm-level employment, not in relation to the plants visited.

[59] The authors would not rule out a closer correspondence in average proportions qualifying at the various levels were the average company sizes more comparable across the two countries.

[60] For more on the differences in the routes to, and typical content of, such qualifications, see the work of our colleague: SJ Prais, Qualified Manpower in Engineering: Britain and other industrially advanced economies, *National Institute Economic Review* (Feb 1998), pp. 76-83.

7

Competitive strategies

Manufacturers in both countries spoke repeatedly of the need to find ways to maintain market share in the face of growing - and increasingly quality-conscious - competition, as European producers recognise that their high wage costs mean their products must compete on world markets in wider terms than mere functionality.

Nowhere were the differences in production strategies of these two countries more evident than in discussions regarding the impact of Far East competition. For the typical British manufacturer, the increased export activity of countries such as South Korea, Taiwan, Thailand and, increasingly, China, is seen as a considerable source of direct competition. That competition, it should be remembered, is not simply limited to the domestic market, but manifests itself also in the European markets (where, at least until recently, sales of unbranded 'own brand' and boxed sets of 'everydayware' to variety stores and supermarkets traditionally provided considerable demand for the output of high volume British earthenware suppliers). More importantly, it has become increasingly fierce in the UK's traditionally important export market of the US, where the shipping times from Far Eastern suppliers, we were told, are now virtually indistinguishable from those of UK manufacturers and where the quality standards attained by these low-wage suppliers have improved to the extent that the cost-advantage has now become a meaningful consideration.

Complaints about competition from these sources were not made in Germany - doubtless in part due to the historical differences in the main markets for German-produced output, but doubtless also due in large part to German perceptions as to the market at which they should be aiming. Few see any profitable future in trying to produce everydayware - known, perhaps tellingly, in the UK as the 'volume' market, but in Germany as *Stapelware* - to compete with imports from low-cost producers. In brief, despite higher actual levels of import penetration, German firms are less vociferous about the effects of low-wage country competition precisely because they do not consider them a *direct* source of competition.

The German objective of offering high quality products to those most likely to buy them leads to a high degree of attention being paid to differentiation of the various consumer groups, and to careful planning as to which ranges to target at which groups. The strategy, while not absent in our British sample, seemed to us somewhat less developed – the typical British manufacturer preferring instead 'to design for design's sake and let the range sell where it sells'.

7.1 Product differentiation

The greater attention to market segmentation among German producers enables the typical manufacturer there to consider separately the needs of his various customer groups and differentiate ('streamline') each product range accordingly - for instance, leaving out tea-, or rather, coffee-pots in all but the most expensive, elegant ranges (since the German customer now typically substitutes this with a vacuum jug); or reducing the typical number of components for a 'fashion-conscious' dinner service to around 30 – rather than the 50-60 for the more elegant, once-in-a-lifetime lines - in line with casual dining trends. In Britain, by contrast, we detected a notable dichotomy in the ranges produced by the firms in our sample – with a large group (accounting for roughly half of total employment in our firms) concentrating on the production of a very narrow range of tableware components (often in 20- and 30-piece boxed sets), while the other half felt it necessary to design and offer *for each range* the full range of crockery and accessories – cruet sets, sauce and gravy boats, a full range of serving bowls – in order to remain (perhaps more in the eyes of the retail buyers than in those of the consumer?) 'in the quality stakes'.

7.2 Customer service

Producers in both countries spoke repeatedly of the need to improve customer service – with greater degrees of customisation (particularly important for producers of hotelware) and more flexible delivery arrangements (tighter delivery dates, smaller orders taken, flexible shipments, etc). This has led to large increases in stocks of semi-finished whitewares in both countries, particularly among the smaller manufacturers, where the ability to produce 'within days' is constrained by the technology typically used. While the higher demand for whitewares as finished goods in Germany probably makes quick delivery an easier proposition, it seems this is an area in which Britain wishes to excel. But there is a there is a considerable obstacle hindering the British manufacturer's ability to respond quickly to repeat orders – namely, the great (excessive?) catalogue of surface designs offered here. As part of their efforts towards customer service, it seems, British manufacturers offer considerably longer guarantees to supply replacements. Two of our British sample of manufacturers, for example, were proud of their record of *never* [having] killed a pattern'. This resulted in their holding, on average, some 6-8 weeks' worth of finished wares in store so as to meet tight (self-imposed) delivery targets of next day or same week dispatch for domestic orders. These same firms were happy to supply typical shipment of 'three cartons' (ie, 60 pieces). The typical German producer, meanwhile, seems to hold less stock (perhaps 3-4 weeks' worth of production as whiteware, generally of the most frequently ordered items only), but considers a timescale of 95 per cent of orders within 10 working days a more realistic target.

7.3 Mass customisation

While a new form or unusual shape may command a premium of some 30-60 per cent, manufacturers face a difficult decision: Whether to seek to compete in the realms of 'difficult manufacturing'; or to try to reduce production costs through product re-design. From our interviews with production managers in the two countries, it seemed that rather greater attention was paid to the latter approach in the UK, with the typical British tableware producer looking increasingly to *re-engineer* his product to *remove* many of the more difficult - eg, turning, milling, etc - operations since more complex shapes render more difficult - and more costly – the use of mass production technology. By contrast, the typical German manufacturer seeks precisely to *increase* the degree of complexity of his output since 'difficult to make is also difficult to copy'. To be clear on the difference, the aim is to design with a high degree of differentiation in mind, whilst simultaneously seeking to reduce the batch sizes required for automation. This higher degree of product differentiation is manifested in both smaller average batch sizes (see p.34 above) and shorter sales runs (around 8-12 years in Germany for the more 'classic' lines; 1-3 years for the more fashion-conscious lines). The aim in Germany is rather to supply the more quality-conscious and aspirational purchasers of dinnerware – that is, those willing to pay a premium price for a more unusual product. Thus, despite the enduring opportunities (for the time being, at least) in the German manufacturers' traditional markets to continue to generate considerable turnover based on sales of whitewares, manufacturers there now look increasingly to move also into the production of shorter runs of *decorated* tableware, while many of the smaller and medium-sized British manufacturers bemoan the loss of their traditional markets for undecorated 'blanks'.

7.4 Optimal inputs

According to those in the trade, three aspects are of overriding importance for the production of quality tableware: good raw materials; good kiln control; and a flexible workforce. In the first of these it seems, Britain has a clear advantage in international terms – perhaps even over Germany - in being close to the source of high quality raw materials. The quality of English clays is universally acknowledged as particularly good. And the proximity of European producers generally to high-quality clays should offer both countries a considerable cost advantage in this respect over many of the lower-cost producers, who, it seems, are often forced to ship out raw materials from Europe in order to achieve comparable output qualities.

In terms of kiln control, sophisticated fast-firing equipment is now widely available. These new kilns are expensive – equal to the typical investment budgets of a year or more for many smaller producers. But their advances offer a considerable advantages in terms of both higher first-quality yields and considerably reduced through-put times.

It is perhaps in the area of worker flexibility that the differential between Britain and Germany is at its greatest. To state the dilemma facing manufacturers somewhat poignantly, the tableware-producing industries of both countries can hardly be described as anything other than mature. As such, the production techniques and technologies – at least, for all but the very largest producers in each country – are largely known *and available worldwide*. Increasing quality levels among low-cost producers thus leave few options open to the higher wage suppliers of Western Europe, other than to seek to supply a more differentiated product range with a high degree of exclusivity in a timely fashion. These requirements in turn imply a considerable degree of flexibility in the manufacturing process. Success depends crucially on having competent craftsmen capable of ensuring that production runs smoothly, with the minimum of rejects and disruption during changeovers, and without the need for excessive numbers of production workers.

7.5 Skills for high quality production

The greater availability of – or rather, reliance on – larger numbers of skilled engineering crews in the German plants seen in our sample is undoubtedly in large part a response to the combined needs of ever more frequent re-setting and re-tooling of machines, a greater customisation of standardised machinery (and machine tools) and a greater need for *reliability* in the smooth running of equipment so as to ensure that bottlenecks in the production process do not occur. Among the largest producers we visited – those with the order books large enough for developing and investing large sums (and regularly) in the most advanced technologies – the ratios of these highly-skilled technicians at factory floor level look set to rise from the current 5-10 per cent to around half of total shopfloor employment, with a large share of that proportional increase reflecting an absolute reduction in the numbers of unskilled production workers employed. Yet, the smaller and medium-sized producers in Germany also predicted proportionately greater requirements for skilled engineers in the future, albeit at lower proportions overall, as the batch sizes for automation continue to decline. Similarly, the higher technical skills required to implement strategies of increased product differentiation and ever-quicker responses to changes in consumer tastes – both at the design level, as well in terms of larger numbers of skilled mould cutters - were also more in evidence in Germany than in the British plants.

Manufacturers in both countries talked consistently of the need for greater 'multi-skilling'; but, from what we have seen in practice, it seems that what is meant by the term varies greatly across the countries. To German managers, multi-skilling in this industry tends to be viewed in terms of the production operative's ability to carry out a wide range of direct making *and peripheral* functions (eg, forming *and* scraping *and* wiping out), and to change between forms routinely and quickly, and usually several times a day. In Britain, by contrast, production workers were typically expected to change the model they were producing, often only once or twice a week, and were generally responsible for only one operation (forming *or* scraping *or* wiping out). In terms of functional flexibility it seems, there is still considerable scope before Britain reaches German levels of labour productivity.

8

Summary and policy conclusions

This investigation involved detailed plant level observations and wider firm-level discussions with a range of 23 tableware manufacturers in Britain and Germany. The sector was chosen as illustrative of a number of older - in economist's terms, 'mature' - manufacturing industries, with largely known technologies and techniques. While both countries have been subject to ever-growing global competition in product markets, Britain and Germany remain the two largest tableware producers in Europe.

Official data from each country's national statistical agency - collected as part of the annual Census of Production - suggest little difference in the relative size and capacity in the two countries. Estimates of relative performance, based on these sources, suggest virtual parity in productivity levels in Britain and Germany in 1998 (the latest year for which official data are available), at market exchange rates.

Comparing performance in *matched plants* in Britain and Germany, this study found productivity – both in terms of output value *and* value added per employee - to be around one third higher in the German plants visited than in Britain. In terms of *quantities* produced, *physical* output per head was actually lower in the German plants than in Britain, with the average German employee producing only around 70 per cent of the annual output volume - ie, number of pieces - of his British counterpart. In terms of *output quality* however, average unit values per item produced in the German plants were 88 per cent higher than each piece made in the UK.

In terms of *quality specialisation*, top-quality grades - defined on the basis of a combination of physical and aesthetic characteristics - accounted for roughly 60 per cent of German production, with very little output in the lowest quality grade. British tableware production, meanwhile, varies more considerably, with around a third of total production aimed at the higher-quality segments of the market (roughly 35 per cent of total volume), while a larger proportion is composed of standard and basic quality wares, which compete for customers in the cost-conscious 'volume' market.

A comparison of a large sample of matched items - dinner plates - sold in the two countries using hedonic regression analysis suggests that a large number of quality dimensions have an impact on the price at which output is sold, but that price alone is an inadequate proxy measure of output quality. From this analysis, based *on quantifiable characteristics only*, it seems that the additional quality attributes embodied in the average plate produced in Germany result in a 25 per cent price premium over British-made output.

Comparing the full range of quality attributes of dinner plates by means of quality-equivalence matching (that is, including quality aspects which were not well-captured by means of a binary variable), revealed that the average German-made plate typically encompasses additional physical and stylistic features valued by the market at around 35 per cent above that of the average British-made product.

Despite the vastly differing approaches used for these two analyses, a broadly consistent conclusion emerges: that of a marked - 25-35 per cent - quality-advantage of the average German-made plate over the average unit produced in the UK. The conclusion is similar in direction, although somewhat lower in magnitude to this Institute's earlier findings of an average 65 per cent quality differential in Germany's favour across a different range of consumer products manufactured in the two countries.

The higher average output quality of German-made plates examined in this study was achieved through a combination of: (1) greater attention to a more exclusive product – with, for instance, smaller batch-sizes (9,000 plates in Germany, 14,200 in the UK, on average) at the clay-forming stage; (2) the production of a more robust product – for instance, greater chip-resistance; and (3) greater emphasis on faultless finishing.

Thus, of the 88 per cent German premium per item produced, some 35 percentage points (that is, roughly 40 per cent of the total differential) can be attributed to a *direct* quality advantage plate-for-plate. But there are also *indirect* quality differences at work, which help to explain the remaining 60 per cent of the higher observed German unit values reported, most notably: compositional differences in the total *output-mixes* of the firms visited - including a lower proportion of the simpler-to-produce flatware items (including plates) in the total output-mix of the German plants than in Britain (52 and 65 per cent, respectively, for the plants in our sample); and, within each of the various types of output (flatware, hollowware, etc), a *greater variety* of items, shapes or forms produced.

Comparisons of cross-country performance using quality-adjusted purchasing power parities (PPPs) suggest that the German *real* productivity advantage is substantially greater than that suggested by market exchange rates. At the industry level of household ceramics producers (that is, including the production of sanitaryware and ceramic tiles), Germany's productivity advantage rises to around 30 per cent over Britain; within the narrowly-defined sub-sector of tableware, the German advantage over Britain rises to some 65 per cent.

Five areas in particular were highlighted as showing notable differences in operation - and contributing to the observed productivity differential - between the countries. In brief:

- A more integrated approach to investment decisions in Germany, with a greater emphasis on working (often with manufacturers) to design the appropriate technology for perceived production needs, and a greater willingness for firms of all sizes to buy in the *associated know-how* for the optimal operation of new equipment.

- The considerable shop-floor experience and technical understanding of the members of the design team in Germany leads to *company-specific* developments of new patterns and forms, with the firm's own technical capabilities in mind. This, coupled with the a greater reliance on skilled tool-makers (mould-cutters), is particularly important in explaining the ability of the firms to produce smaller batches of high-quality and heavily differentiated products.

- Proportionately more skilled maintenance technicians employed within the German firms than in the UK, and a greater reliance on *electrical* engineering skills (as opposed to mechanical and tool-making skills, as in the UK). Such skills are viewed as of paramount importance – both for the frequent re-setting and routine maintenance of production equipment, as well as for the customisation of standardised technology to meet the optimal production needs of the firm's unique product mix.

- A significantly greater proportion of the supervisory personnel and foremen in the German plants held formal vocational qualifications than in the British plants (at 50 and 20 per cent, respectively). The German foremen seemed better prepared to assume a more varied combination of supervisory roles – from production scheduling to planning the routine maintenance of equipment, as well as to foreseeing and troubleshooting potential problems in producing a new range *before* that range goes into production. The role of the typical foreman in the British plants, meanwhile, tends to be limited to ensuring that production schedules *handed down from above* are met, or to reporting to the factory management the problems in trying to meet those schedules once production has begun.

- Greater functional flexibility among production operatives in the German plants, requiring fewer peripheral workers (1 in 14 of all shopfloor workers in Germany, compared to 1 in 9 in the British plants), which contributed directly to Germany's higher output per head. Moreover, the greater ability of German operatives to switch between models more quickly undoubtedly contributes in no small way to the German firm's ability to achieve a *greater degree of differentiation* of output.

Our sample is small – just two dozen or so producers in the two countries; undoubtedly a larger study – and of a broader range of industries - would prove useful. In the meantime, our investigations in the tableware industry suggests an important policy lesson of benefit to a large range of *mature* industries. In terms of both industrial and training policy, it seems that there is rather more to be gained from enhanced efforts aimed at increasing the availability of the higher-level maintenance, tool-making and production engineering skills essential to the smooth operation of modern production methods and technologies, than in further efforts to certify by means of low-level qualifications the routine operations carried out by the majority of production-line workers.

Appendix A

Ceramic tableware: background information

A.1 Output, employment and productivity

Data in official publications are available on a roughly comparable basis for industry 26.21, household and miscellaneous ceramic goods.[61] These data can only be derived on a consistent basis from 1993, following major revisions to the UK standard industrial classification, and even from then there remain some statistical problems in mapping trends over time in both countries.[62] Nevertheless the trends as shown in Table A.1 below do give a reasonably accurate broad picture of conditions in the industry.

Table A.1. shows output, employment and productivity growth from 1993 to 1998 in the two countries. Over this period real output has been declining at roughly the same rate in both countries, at an average annual rate of 1.5% in this five year period. Employment has been falling considerably faster in Germany, consistent with observations in the main text that German firms have been substituting capital for labour at a greater rate than in Britain. The net effect is labour productivity growth rates on average in Germany about twice those experienced in Britain.

Table A.1: Trends in output, employment and labour productivity, UK and Germany (% per annum)

	Real Sales	Employment	Labour Productivity*
1993-98			
UK	-1.48	-4.54	3.06
Germany	-1.51	-8.59	7.08

Sources: Germany: *Produzierendes Gewerbe, Fachserie 4, Reihe, 4.1.1., Beschaftigung, Umsatz und Energieversorgung der Unternehmen und Betreibe des Verarbeitenden Gewerbe*, Statistisches Bundesamt, annual publications, 1993 to 1998. UK: *Annual Census of Production, 1997*, Office for National Statistics and sources as for Table 1 for 1998.

A.2 Consumer expenditure patterns

It is even more difficult to derive consistent estimates of consumer expenditure, valued at retail prices, on ceramic tableware in the two countries since the definition of the product area changes from one publication to another.[63] Nevertheless the available data suggests that in 1998 sales of ceramic tableware were about 30% higher in Germany than in the UK.[64] There are variations across the two countries in the type of product consumed. Thus in 1998 per capita sales of <u>China and Porcelain</u> housewares was 50% higher in Germany than in the UK but per capita values sold of <u>other ceramic housewares</u> was about 70% higher in Britain, than in Germany. Within Europe the UK values per capita of china and porcelain tablware are among the lowest, while France, Belgium and Austria rank among the highest consumers. On the other hand, per capita consumption of other ceramic housewares in the UK was second highest in Europe with only Norway consuming more.

Over time, estimates by Mintel suggest about a 2.4% annual average rise in the value of china and earthenware sales in the UK from 1993 to 1998, representing virtually no change in real terms once allowance is made for increases in the products sold.[65] Similarly available publications for Germany suggest no real change in consumption over this period.[66]

A.3 International trade

Table 1 of the text showed trade balances for industry 26.21. For the purposes of this study it is more appropriate to consider tableware alone, i.e. excluding ornaments and giftware. In 1998 both Britain and Germany enjoyed a positive trade balance in ceramic tableware and household articles. UK exports were more than double the value of imports and were considerably greater than German exports measured in £ Sterling. German exports were only about 30% higher than imports.[67] Looking at product category, bone china and porcelain dominate German trade, accounting for 90% of exports and a smaller 60% of imports – in fact Germany had a trade deficit in ceramic household goods manufactured from materials other than china and porcelain. Tableware from china and porcelain accounts for a marginally smaller share of UK exports than other forms and accounts for only about 45% of imports.

Measured in £ sterling, Germany exported more tableware of china and porcelain than did Britain but also imported more of this category. In total, EU markets accounted for a greater proportion of German export trade than was the case for the UK but the EU's share of German imports was lower than in Britain. However in absolute terms German exports to and imports from the EU of products of china and porcelain were considerably greater than in Britain.

Table A.2: International trade in ceramic tableware and household articles, 1998

	Exports		Imports		Trade Balance
	£ mill	% to EU	£ mill	% from EU	£ mill
A. UK (£ mill)					
Tableware of China & Porcelain	131.2	23.9	39.9	44.5	91.3
Tableware of other kinds of pottery	167.7	45.0	75.7	45.4	92.0
TOTAL	298.9	35.7	115.5	45.1	183.4
B. Germany (DM mill)					
Tableware of China & Porcelain	199.8	55.4	106.6	29.5	93.2
Tableware of other kinds of Pottery	21.6	51.5	69.5	47.4	-47.9
TOTAL	221.5	55.0	176.1	36.6	45.3

Source: *International Trade by Commodities Statistics, Revision 2, 1990-1999*, OECD, Paris.

More detail on the geographic origin of trade is presented in Table A.3. It shows clearly the dominance of the US as a single country for UK exports and its relative unimportance for German exporters.[68] In both countries exports to the rest of Europe is dominated by EU partner countries although former Eastern European countries represent a significant share of German exports. Over a quarter of UK exports go to Asia, but primarily to Japan which again is a small market for German exports.

A somewhat different pattern emerges when we examine the geographic source of imports. In 1998 nearly half imports to the UK came from Asia, with Thailand, China, Chinese Taipei and Indonesia being the most important sources within Asia. On the other hand, although Asia is an important source of imports for Germany, it is the former Eastern European countries which constitute the biggest threat, particularly in the porcelain and china segment of the market.

Table A.3: World import and export shares by region and country, 1998

	Exports			Imports		
	China and Porcelain	Other forms	Total	China and Porcelain	Other forms	Total
A. UK						
Region: Europe	**27.3**	**51.4**	**40.9**	**56.2**	**46.7**	**50.0**
Germany	3.8	5.4	4.7	11.5	1.8	5.1
France	2.7	5.2	4.1	10.6	2.2	5.1
Italy	6.3	5.0	5.6	7.1	12.9	10.9
Netherlands	2.3	7.9	5.4	1.8	1.1	1.3
Portugal	0.4	0.7	0.5	5.0	21.8	16.0
Czech Republic	0.0	0.5	0.3	2.0	0.0	0.7
Poland	0.2	0.3	0.3	4.8	0.1	1.7
Region: North America	**34.9**	**33.3**	**34.0**	**4.8**	**1.8**	**2.8**
USA	*28.4*	*27.6*	*28.0*	*4.6*	*1.4*	*2.5*
Region: Asia	**29.5**	**8.8**	**17.9**	**37.9**	**50.7**	**46.3**
Bangladesh	0.0	0.0	0.0	3.4	0.9	1.8
China	0.0	0.0	0.0	9.3	8.9	9.1
Indonesia	0.1	0.0	0.0	5.9	4.8	5.2
Japan	22.7	3.2	11.7	4.9	1.1	2.4
Philippines	0.0	0.0	0.0	2.3	1.6	1.8
Thailand	0.0	0.0	0.0	3.6	16.2	11.8
Chinese Taipei	0.7	0.2	0.4	1.3	13.9	9.6
Region: Other World	**8.3**	**6.5**	**7.2**	**1.1**	**0.8**	**0.9**
B. Germany						
Region: Europe	**79.7**	**75.1**	**79.2**	**75.8**	**59.2**	**69.1**
UK	3.3	4.1	3.4	2.9	5.8	4.1
France	5.4	5.2	5.4	2.1	2.9	3.0
Italy	14.2	5.8	13.4	3.2	17.3	8.9
Netherlands	5.7	6.7	5.8	1.0	3.0	1.8
Portugal	0.4	0.4	0.4	3.0	15.6	8.1
Czech Republic	12.5	3.8	11.6	31.5	2.0	19.6
Poland	0.6	4.2	1.0	8.3	2.9	6.2
Region: North America	**7.1**	**15.9**	**8.0**	**0.4**	**0.4**	**0.4**
USA	*6.6*	*15.4*	*7.5*	*0.4*	*0.4*	*0.4*
Region: Asia	**11.0**	**7.4**	**10.6**	**23.2**	**39.5**	**29.8**
Bangladesh	0.0	0.0	0.0	0.0	0.1	0.1
China	0.0	0.0	0.0	11.9	17.4	14.1
Indonesia	0.0	0.0	0.0	2.4	0.7	1.7
Japan	5.0	1.7	4.7	1.9	1.5	1.7
Philippines	0.0	0.0	0.0	1.6	0.5	1.1
Thailand	0.0	0.0	0.0	1.0	3.8	2.1
Chinese Taipei	0.3	0.4	0.3	1.6	10.7	5.3
Region: Other World	**2.3**	**1.6**	**2.2**	**0.6**	**0.9**	**0.7**

Source: as for Table A.2

Finally it is useful to examine the time series pattern of trade in the two countries. To abstract from exchange rate movements, Table A.4. shows the value of trade in both countries from 1993 to 1998 in domestic currencies. In nominal terms, overall the value of UK exports increased by only aan average rate of 1.6% per annum between 1993 and 1998. The value of UK exports peaked in 1997 with a significant reduction of about 16% in the following year. This compared to average annual increases of about 14% in the years 1993 to 1997. In percentage terms the greatest reduction between 1997 and 1998 was in china and porcelain, largely due to significant reductions in exports to the US (a fall of about 10%) and to Japan (a large reduction of about 35%) with little change in exports to European countries.

In the same five year period UK imports increased by an average rate of over 9% per annum, primarily from Asian countries and more concentrated in products manufactured from materials other than porcelain and china. Thus this period was one of a declining trade surpluses in Britain from about £200 million in 1993 to £180 million in 1998.

German exports showed no significant growth over the period 1993 to 1998, although the time pattern was somewhat different than in Britain. Thus there was a large decline from 1993 to 1994 followed by increases thereafter – from 1994 to 1998 German exports grew by an average rate of about 2% per annum with the growth rate being lower in porcelain and china than other products.[69] German imports increased at an average rate of over 4% in total from 1993 to 1995, lower than in Britain but import growth in porcelain and china was higher at about 8% per annum. This came largely though growth in porcelain and china imports from the Czech republic (a massive rise of 30% per annum) and Poland (an equally impressive rise of 17% per annum). Asian imports of porcelain and china rose by less than 1% per annum. Germany's trade surplus declined from DM 230 million in 1993 to about DM 130 million in 1998.

Finally Table A.5 shows trends by type of product, distinguishing intra and extra EU trade. The shares of UK exports accounted for by bone china and porcelain have increased since 1993, but declined between 1996 and 1998, due entirely to a fall in the share of this product in Extra-EU exports. Earthenware has become less important in total UK exports, particularly in Extra-EU markets but stoneware has become more important primarily in the EU. German exports are dominated by the bone china and porcelain product area – this product group has shown some small decline in EU markets but has increased in importance in markets outside the EU.

Table A.4: Imports and exports in national currencies, 1993-98

	Exports			Imports		
	China & Porcelain	Other forms	Total	China & Porcelain	Other forms	Total
A. UK (£mill)						
1993	130.3	145.7	275.9	33.8	38.5	72.4
1994	*159.4*	*163.9*	*323.3*	*36.1*	*55.0*	*91.1*
1995	163.6	177.8	341.4	37.7	55.7	93.5
1996	184.3	193.0	377.3	39.9	71.0	110.8
1997	166.9	185.1	352.0	35.7	71.7	107.4
1998	131.2	167.7	298.9	39.9	75.7	115.5
B. Germany (DM mill)						
1993	580.1	65.8	645.9	204.9	208.7	413.6
1994	*537.8*	*55.0*	*592.8*	*215.9*	*179.3*	*395.2*
1995	541.7	54.8	596.5	225.2	180.6	405.8
1996	537.5	57.3	594.8	252.1	192.9	445.0
1997	583.6	63.4	647.0	284.2	215.6	499.9
1998	583.8	63.2	647.1	311.4	203.2	514.5

Source: As for Table A.2

In terms of competition from imports to the UK, the largest increase has been in earthenware from EU countries and stoneware from outside the EU.[70] Imports of bone china and porcelain have decreased in importance over time. On the other hand in Germany imports of china and porcelain have increased in importance. Thus Germany is facing increased competition, in particular from outside the EU, in the product area where its production is concentrated. Britain is facing more severe competition in the lower end (earthenware and stoneware) of its market.

Table A.5:   Trade shares by product group, selected years, 1993-1998

	Total			Intra-EU			Extra-EU		
	1993	1996	1998	1993	1996	1998	1993	1996	1998
I. EXPORTS									
A. UK									
Tableware of China									
& Porcelain	35.3	46.5	41.4	20.7	27.7	28.0	46.5	56.7	49.2
Tableware &									
household articles of									
Common Pottery	3.2	1.8	2.8	3.8	2.1	3.1	2.7	1.6	2.7
Tableware &									
household articles									
of Stoneware	6.3	8.4	12.1	6.5	10.0	14.3	6.1	7.6	10.8
Tableware &									
household articles									
of earthenware									
& fine china	53.0	41.1	41.0	67.5	59.0	53.6	41.8	31.4	33.8
Other ceramic									
tableware &									
household articles	2.3	2.2	2.6	1.4	1.2	0.9	3.0	2.7	3.6
TOTAL	100	100	100	100	100	100	100	100	100
B. Germany									
Tableware of									
China & Porcelain	89.6	90.2	90.1	92.2	91.9	90.7	84.5	87.9	89.3
Tableware &									
household articles									
of Common Pottery	1.1	1.2	1.0	0.8	0.9	0.6	1.7	1.6	1.5
Tableware &									
household articles									
of Stoneware	4.9	3.9	3.8	3.7	3.2	3.8	7.3	4.8	3.8
Tableware &									
household articles									
of earthenware									
& fine china	3.9	4.1	4.3	3.0	3.5	4.4	5.7	4.8	4.2
Other ceramic									
tableware &									
household articles	0.5	0.7	0.9	0.3	0.6	0.6	0.7	0.9	1.3
TOTAL	100	100	100	100	100	100	100	100	100

Source as for Table A.2

Table A.5 continued: Trade shares by product group, selected years, 1993-1998

	Total			Intra-EU			Extra-EU		
	1993	1996	1998	1993	1996	1998	1993	1996	1998
II. IMPORTS									
A. UK									
Tableware of China & Porcelain	44.9	34.6	33.2	42.9	34.8	33.1	47.8	34.3	33.3
Tableware & household articles of Common Pottery	4.7	4.9	5.8	4.5	6.7	6.8	5.1	2.9	4.9
Tableware & household articles of Stoneware	15.9	22.0	26.0	14.6	6.8	11.7	18.0	39.3	37.8
Tableware & household articles of earthenware & fine china	24.8	32.2	28.6	26.8	44.6	41.6	21.8	18.2	17.9
Other ceramic tableware & household articles	9.7	6.3	6.4	11.2	7.1	6.7	7.4	5.3	6.1
TOTAL	100	100	100	100	100	100	100	100	100
B. Germany									
Tableware of China & Porcelain	49.0	55.7	60.1	47.5	44.9	48.4	50.6	62.8	66.7
Tableware & household articles of Common Pottery	4.6	5.3	4.1	6.6	9.2	7.1	2.5	2.7	2.4
Tableware & household articles of Stoneware	16.7	16.5	14.6	6.6	6.6	5.4	27.1	23.1	19.9
Tableware & household articles of earthenware & fine china	26.1	18.8	17.1	34.4	32.0	30.3	17.6	10.0	9.6
Other ceramic tableware & household articles	3.6	3.7	4.1	4.9	7.3	8.8	2.3	1.3	1.5
TOTAL	100	100	100	100	100	100	100	100	100

Source as for Table A.2

Notes

[61] Germany: *Produzierendes Gewerbe, Fachserie 4, Reihe, 4.1.1., Beschaftigung, Umsatz und Energieversorgung der Unternehmen und Betreibe des Verarbeitenden Gewerbe*, Statistisches Bundesamt, annual publications, 1993 to 1998. UK: *Annual Census of Production, 1997*, Office for National Statistics and sources as for Table 1 for 1998.

[62] These include problems caused by the unification of Germany, minor industry reclassifications in Germany in 1995 and inconsistent sources for UK data in 1998 relative to previous years. Rough adjustment factors were employed to allow for these problems.

[63] Thus some publications cover all ceramic goods including sanitary ware and ornaments while other refer largely to tableware.

[64] *Consumer Europe*, 1999/2000, Euromonitor PLC, London.

[65] Mintel: *Market Intelligence Report: China and Earthenware*, May 1998.

[66] Based on data in Retail Intelligence, *'Retailing in Germany'*, *Corporate Intellegence Report*, London, 2000.

[67] Note the German trade deficit reported in Table 1 of the main text comes about as a result of a very large deficit in ornaments and giftware. Similarly the UK surplus for tableware is much larger than that for the industry as a whole.

[68] The latter could be interpreted positively as Germany being less dependent than Britain on one market or negatively as German inability to make significant inroads into the richest market in the world.

[69] These trends are of course dependent on cyclical changes. Starting in 1992 however makes no difference to the conclusions but Germany looks better than Britain if the beginning period were 1994.

[70] Note, the distinction between earthenware and stoneware is somewhat blurred so similar products could be traded across these two groups.

Appendix B

Methods to estimate relative quality in ceramic tableware in the UK and Germany

In estimating relative productivity or relative consumption in Britain and Germany it is necessary to take account of the possibility that the quality of the goods may vary across the two countries. Quality differences are extremely difficult to measure accurately. A common approach employed to get at quality differences is to adjust cross country price ratios of clearly defined products for quality dimensions and then use the results to deflate the ratios of the values in domestic currencies of output or consumption.

A first step in this process is to choose a product for comparison in the two countries. In this study we have used a standard sized (26/27cm) dinner plate as representative of ceramic tableware. The second step is to delineate the quality dimensions of this product – this was based on the discussion of quality dimensions in the main text above. We first present a brief discussion of different methodologies. This is followed by a consideration of the results of the adjustments for quality based on retail (consumption) prices of plates. Finally this Chapter includes a discussion of adjustments to the basic methodology that might be necessary to move from consumption to production price ratios.

B.1 Methodologies to take account of quality differences

A number of different approaches have been used in the literature. Here we compare the results using four methods, i. Unit value ratios; ii. Matched products; iii. Hedonic regressions; and iv. Quality rankings. Methods iii and iv were briefly described in Chapter 3 of the main text. This Appendix includes considerably more detail on methods and results and contrasts these with methods i and ii which we consider to be less useful in the context of ceramic tableware.

Unit value ratios

This technique starts from total production (or consumption) and divides this into various categories, distinguishing quality dimensions. For each category sales values are divided by quantities produced to yield unit values which can be compared across countries. These are then aggregated using quantity weights in the two countries. If sufficient categories can be delineated then this approach can yield an estimate that is based on a more representative sample than is usually the case with matched price models. Suppose there are j separate categories with quantities denoted by q and sales values by V and let G and U denote Germany and the UK respectively. Then the unit values of product j are given by:

$$p_j^G = V_j^G/q_j^G \quad \text{and} \quad p_j^U = V_j^U/q_j^U$$

The unit value ratio, in DM/£, is calculated as:

$$UVR = (P^{qG} * P^{qU})^{0.5}$$

where $\quad P^{qG} = \Sigma_j p_j^G q_j^G / \Sigma_j p_j^U q_j^G$

and $\quad P^{qG} = \Sigma_j p_j^G q_j^U / \Sigma_j p_j^U q_j^U$

Thus the unit value ratio is calculated as the geometric mean of the sum of German quantity weighted unit values and UK quantity weighted unit values. This method has been applied in a large number of studies of international comparisons of productivity.[71]

There are a number of problems with the unit value approach. The first is that it may not be possible, given the data, to delineate very many quality dimensions. A second problem is that the measure of quantity may not be meaningful in the context of the product being compared. Finally the unit values being compared may refer to a wide mixture of products. In the specific case of ceramic tableware the available data only allow division by one quality dimension, body paste. Also the quantity measure available in the published data is physical weight (kg) which is only useful if average weight does not vary according to body paste. In fact the latter is not generally true – porcelain and bone china tend to be lighter than earthenware which in turn is lighter than stoneware. Finally the categories available refer to all kitchenware and some sanitary ware and so the results will depend on the mix of these products. For example, this method could be comparing mainly dining ware in one country with a higher concentration of oven-to–tableware in another. In general the unit value approach works best when comparing product areas which are reasonably homogeneous. This is unlikely to be the case in ceramic tableware.

Matched products

The most commonly used approach to allow for quality differences across countries, and that employed by Eurostat in computing their consumption purchasing power parities (PPPs) is the matched price model. In this approach a sample of prices of identical goods are compared in the two countries and then aggregated to yield an overall price ratio. In theory this method should yield a quality adjusted PPP. In practice it suffers from a number of limitations. Chief of these is the question of how *representative* are the matched products of the goods actually sold in the two countries. The matched product method works well for products where tastes are similar in the two countries, e.g. computers. But in general in consumer goods it is difficult to find identical products sold in both countries.

In the specific case of ceramic tableware the differences in tastes outlined in Chapter 3 of the main text above resulted in matches in product areas which served a minority consumption demand in one of the two countries. Thus it was difficult to match earthenware popular in Britain with identical products in Germany and many porcelain products sold in Germany with identical products sold in Britain. In fact most matches were for products at the high end of the market in both countries, produced by manufacturers with a recognised international brand name. Thus in the specific case of ceramic tableware the matched prices are unlikely to be representative of the majority of consumer demand in either country.

A second problem with this approach is the question of how to aggregate the individual matched price quotations to achieve an overall price ratio. In theory the prices should be weighted by quantities produced (or sold) in the two countries but this information is not available at the required level of detail for detailed product areas such as ceramic tableware. Thus it is common practice to merely use an unweighted average of the price quotations.

Hedonic regressions

This approach is based on a sample of prices of products in the two countries where it is possible for researchers to record a range of quality dimensions. The price of the product is then regressed on these quality dimensions with the constant in the regression representing the estimated quality adjusted price. With a large enough sample and sufficient detail on quality dimensions this technique is potentially very useful. A large sample size, based on pooling the observations in the two countries, gets over the problem of representativity. This method can also take account of a high number of quality dimensions, so long as they are easily observable by the researchers. It also has the advantage that the method yields information on the extent to which individual quality aspects affect price. However there may be aspects of quality which are not easy to define within this approach. In the specific context of ceramic tableware this method proved to be a useful approach since it was possible to take account of many well defined quality characteristics.

The following regression equation was estimated:

$$\ln(\text{price}) = \alpha_1 DU + \alpha_2 DG + \Sigma_i \beta_i DC_i + e_i$$

where DU is a dummy variable taking the value 1 if the price was observed in the UK, DG equals 1 if the plate was part of the German sample; DC_i are dummy variables representing characteristics and e_i is the error term. In this formulation the coefficients b_i represent the proportionate amount by which price changes according to the quality dimensions. The estimated quality adjusted PPP in DM per £ can be calculated as $\exp(\alpha_2)/\exp(\alpha_1)$.

The estimation was carried out on a sample of 427 observations on the prices and quality characteristics of standard size dinner plates. Details of the sampling methods and summary statistics are presented below. The quality dimensions chosen were a mixture of objective characteristics (such as body paste, degree of decoration) and more subjective criterion (everydayware, trendy, etc) related to the market to which they are aimed.

Body paste was divided into four categories, earthenware, stoneware, porcelain and bone china. Some products were listed as 'fine china' - although most products in this category were close to earthenware; discussions with ceramics experts suggested that this was not invariably the case and 'fine china' can cover a range of body pastes. Given this uncertainty, these products were excluded from the sample, as were products made from 'common pottery' where again there was some uncertainty regarding its exact definition. A second basic distinction is that between undecorated whiteware and plates on which a coloured design was placed. Within the former we distinguished plain white from those which were embossed. In the design category we distinguished between those which were entirely one colour or merely a single coloured rim on a white plate (single design) from more elaborate designs involving shades of one colour or multi-coloured designs (multi-design). For both single and multi-designs we included as a separate dimension whether the plate was gilded defined as including some metal, usually gold but sometimes platinum or silver. Finally, in terms of 'hard characteristics' the method in which the colour was placed on the plate was also included, divided into three categories, 1. hand decorated and/or colour wash, 2. applied by transfer or 3. stamped (colour and design applied by machinery). The first two categories involve labour intensive techniques which add to the cost of production. Although at first sight it may seem that multi-design should generally involve either hand decoration or a transfer this turned out not to be the case. Many seemingly elaborate designs are sprayed onto the plates, an observation which was confirmed in the plant visits.[72]

A number of more subjective quality dimensions were considered. The first was whether the plate was likely to be purchased for everyday use, because it was stylish or as a once in a life time purchase. In terms of production costs, being stylish requires investment in design capabilities whereas manufacturers in the once-off purchase categories generally are required to continue producing this line for some considerable length of time to facilitate replacement purchases. The division of the sample into these three categories was informed by our extensive interviews with retail buyers.[73]

Since brand is an important characteristic in this market, a second 'subjective' dimension was to group plates into those produced by manufacturers whose brand name is considered to be synonymous with quality and those produced by other manufacturers. The quality dimensions offered by branded goods could include such tangible factors as durability, which in turn is related to the quality of the raw ingredients (such as materials in body paste, glazes, % precious metals in gilding etc.) incorporated in the products. But these could also be intangible factors such as research effort devoted to achieving attractive colours and designs. We first grouped those plates produced by manufacturers with an internationally recognised brand name. These products enjoyed a considerable price premium over all others, having allowed for easily observable quality dimensions such as body paste. Although the international brand name undoubtedly conveys some quality information it is likely that they also incorporate other quality dimensions not directly related to production such as fulfilling consumer's desire for exclusivity. The latter in turn is likely to be influenced by the manufacturers' expenditures (both past and present) on intangibles such as advertising and marketing the brand name.

The second group were 'national brands', defined as products which had a particular following in one of the countries, according to retailers we spoke to, but were generally not considered to be brands in the other market. The quality dimensions incorporated in these products are likely to be similar to those for international brands but they are considered to be 'less exclusive'.

Quality rankings

The final method employed was designed to get at quality characteristics not easily observable within the hedonic framework. This was based on discussions with retail buyers on the quality aspects of a sample of plates as delineated in Chapter 3 above. To take an example from ceramic tableware, it was obvious from buyers that there are unobservable differences in a product as simple as a white earthenware plate in terms of dimensions such as how easily the product chips and its general look (whiteness, porosity, glaze) and feel.

This 'quality rankings ' method divided plates into four quality dimensions: top, superior, standard and basic. Each of these categories were delineated separately for decorated and whiteware. The placing of plates into one of these four groups was based on discussions with retail buyers on the quality aspects of a sample of plates. Given the nature of the product (its sheer bulkiness and weight), it was not possible to show the same sample of plates to all buyers while ensuring a sufficiently large and representative sample. Therefore the ranking was undertaken by the researchers based primarily on plates shown to one or more expert together with a few which obviously typified the category (mainly in the basic and whiteware categories in order to increase the sample).

The top category included plates which were categorised by buyers as representing a combination of the highest quality features. These were invariably manufactured either from porcelain or bone china and included general finish, glaze and overall appearance which buyers suggested were among the best products available in the market. Many international brand name products appeared in this category but it also included a number of other high quality products and not all plates produced by the top brand names were included in this top group.

The superior quality plates had many features of top quality but were deemed not quite up to the latter standard as a result of one or more deficiencies in their quality characteristics. But these products did have distinctive features which separated them from standard products. These plates were often produced by national, and in a few cases international, brand name firms but again this was not invariably the case. Standard plates were those which included some quality characteristics but not sufficiently to place them in the superior category. Finally basic plates were those found to be lacking any of the quality features discussed by retail buyers and other experts.

It is important to emphasise that price was not taken into account when grouping the plates. In fact the buyers were not told the origin of the plates until they had discussed their quality attributes. For each category the PPP was calculated as the ratio of the (geometric) average across the prices in the two countries. These PPPs were then weighted by their market shares in each category in the two countries. These shares in turn were based on discussions with buyers, aggregate statistical information and published reports on tableware markets. The PPPs were calculated using both German and UK weights and the overall (common weight) PPP was calculated as the geometric mean of these two. Whiteware was assumed to represent 25% of each UK group and 30% of German, with these ratios again based on market information.

B.2 Estimation results

We first present estimates for consumption PPPs and then consider the issue of how appropriate these are as measures of production price ratios. It would be useful to have an estimate of the relative price of all plates sold in both countries as a benchmark with which to the results below. Such a price is not available. One possible benchmark is the market exchange rate of 3.13 DM/£ at the time when most of the price information was gathered.[74] But this rate is considered by most commentators as being far from an equilibrium exchange rate which would measure overall purchasing power parity in the two countries (due mainly to the abnormally low value of the euro). A second alternative, and the one used as the benchmark in the main text is the GDP purchasing power parity calculated by OECD/Eurostat. This was 3.04 DM/£ in 1998, and 3.01 DM/£ in 1999, somewhat below the market exchange rate.

An alternative is to use information on the sample of plates used in the hedonic regression analysis. The unweighted average prices in the sample for the two countries separately implied a price ratio of 2.55 DM/£. However, as discussed below the sample was not considered to be representative of the quantity weights by characteristic of products sold in the market, particularly when considering division by body paste. Weighting the average prices by the quantity shares of earthenware and stoneware versus porcelain and bone china consumed in the two countries implied a price ratio of 3.16 DM/£ which is close to the actual market exchange rate at that time. The quantity (number of plates) weights in turn were derived using market information on value shares combined with the estimated price differentials in the sample between the two broad body paste categories. An alternative calculation allowing varying proportions of whitewares across the two countries yielded similar results.

Unit value ratios

Quantity and value data were available for 1998 for three categories, 1. porcelain and bone china, 2. earthenware and 3. stoneware.[75] The unit value ratio for total consumption (production plus imports minus exports) was estimated at 2.92 DM/£. This figure was adjusted to 1999 using the growth in the retail price index for household goods in both countries. Thus the 1999 unit value ratio was 2.90 DM/£ which was only marginally below the market exchange rate for that year. This result seems somewhat surprising as it purports to take account of the body paste quality dimension. This should lower the price ratio as German consumption is more concentrated in high priced products. Examination of the unit values for the individual items underlying this calculation, however, shows unit values for earthenware significantly above those for porcelain and china, contrary to expectations based on a detailed examination of the prices of plates. This might occur if heavier items such as serving bowls were more concentrated in earthenware. In turn this suggests that the use of physical weight as a quantity dimension is not very useful.

Matched products

Samples of the prices of plates, together with their quality characteristics were collected in both countries during end 1999. These samples are discussed in detail in the section on hedonic regressions below. An attempt was made to match as many plates as possible in the two countries. For the reasons outlined above this proved to be difficult so that from a total sample of 427 plates we could only match 23. Of these 6 were made from earthenware, 10 from porcelain and 7 from bone china. No stoneware matches were achieved. Summary statistics of the prices, and resulting PPPs are presented in Table B.1.

Table B.1: Prices of matched plates, UK and Germany, 1999

	German Price (DM)	UK price (£)	PPP (DM/£)
Mean	36.9	14.9	2.53
Standard deviation	24.2	9.5	0.46
Maximum	129.0	47.0	3.44
Minimum	4.9	2.0	1.73

Hedonic regressions

This section attempts to analyse the impact of various quality characteristics in determining the price of ceramic tableware. To do so we collected retail prices on a large number of dinner plates and analysed how the prices varied according to a number of quality characteristics. We first outline the details of the sample chosen. This is followed by a preliminary analysis of the extent to which price is affected by changing quality dimensions. We then consider the hedonic regression analysis as a tool for decomposing price variations and for estimating a quality adjusted PPP.

Sample selection

A large number of observations on price and quality indicators were collected on a standard size dinner plate (26cm -27cm) from a sample of retail stores in Britain and Germany in November/December 1999 and Spring 2000. Prices were gathered in three locations in Britain (London, Birmingham and Coventry) and 2 locations in Germany (Frankfurt, and Berlin). The price collection times were chosen as periods when plates were sold at full price and so we can abstract from problems caused by discounting at different rates in different stores.[76] Price did not appear to change with small variations in plate size but 'trendy' large plates of 30cm commanded a higher price. However large plates remain the exception and since we observed very few plates in this size range they were excluded from the analysis.

In total observations were taken from 21 retail outlets in Britain and 8 in Germany, although somewhat more were visited to check if prices varied across regions. In addition we visited a number of specialist china shops, owned by manufacturers to see if they commanded a price premium or if the range of items included in these shops was greater than in the Department stores. In fact in Britain neither was true, the prices were identical in the specialist stores to those in Department stores and the range appeared the same - the latter observation was confirmed by sales assistants in the specialist shops. In Germany prices were occasionally higher in specialist stores – discussions with sales assistants suggested that these stores provide an additional service in obtaining repeat orders and replacements more quickly than Department stores.

In both countries some tableware is sold in dinner services, but these vary by size of sets - and the extent to which each piece in a set is discounted also varies. In most retail outlets individual items were sold along-side dinner services. The exception was the popular catalogue stores which do not carry individual items; in these cases we checked the type and manufacturer of dinner services in the catalogues and found these plates or their equivalent in other retail stores.

The retail outlets chosen covered a wide range of plates from the very cheap to expensive. The sample was however truncated at both ends. At the lower price end, quotations were not taken from discount stores as these were generally production 'seconds'. At the very top end of the market, plates are often exclusive to a single retailer or a small group of retailers, so we also excluded a number of brands with these features.

Very cheap plates (less than £5) accounted for about 28% of the sample and very expensive (more than £20) for about 10%. In the middle ranges plates costing between £5 and £10 accounted for 37%, those between £10 and £15 for 16% and those between £15 and £20 for 9%. There is very little hard evidence on actual price ranges of plates sold in the market as a whole. At the lower end the sample proportions are likely to be smaller than would be consistent with figures quoted for 1997 by Mintel, who estimated that 65% of UK retail sales were in the less than £10 category – only 35% of the total value of the plates included in the UK sample were accounted for plates in the less than £10 range.[77] Against this the sample excludes very high priced plates. On balance it is probably the case that the sample is more concentrated in the middle price ranges than is actual consumption. However we are not overly concerned about this. The purpose of this exercise is to gain insight into quality dimensions of plates purchased by *average* consumers. We are less concerned with very high priced items whose quality dimensions are difficult to comprehend.

The objective was to secure prices for as varied a selection of plates as possible, so as to give sufficient variation in the quality characteristics. To do so it was necessary to include plates produced not only in the UK and Germany, but also from other European and Asian producers. The sample consisted of price observations on plates which differed in at least one quality dimension.[78] This gave a total sample of 282 plates in Britain and 145 in Germany, giving a combined sample of 427 plates.[79] Of the total sample, 256 plates were produced in either the UK or Germany, representing 54% of the UK sample and a larger 72% of the German sample.

It is desirable to ensure the sample is reasonably representative of the characteristics actually consumed in the two countries while at the same time allowing sufficient variation by quality dimension to yield accurate (in the sense of low variance) regression coefficients. We did not attempt to constrain the sample to include a fixed proportion of any characteristic but rather relied on the large sample size to yield a reasonable cross section of the actual consumption patterns of ceramic tableware.

Sample summary statistics

Table B.2 shows the division of the total sample by plate characteristics and the average price in each category. It also shows this information for the two countries separately. In terms of body paste porcelain and earthenware together represented nearly 80% of the sample with bone china being the next most important category. There are large differences in the two countries according to body paste with porcelain dominating the German sample whereas earthenware is the most important category in Britain. Bone china is small in Germany relative to its share in Britain. These divisions by body paste reflect in part the actual pattern of consumption in the two countries but do not totally take account of differences in quantity shares. To do so would have the British sample dominated by earthenware and the German by porcelain at a cost of less variation by body paste with consequent problems for econometric estimation.[80]

Whiteware accounts for just under a quarter of the total sample, with this category representing a marginally greater proportion of the German than the British sample. these differences across countries also appear in aggregate consumption figures (see the discussion in Chapter 3 above). Of decorated ware, about one third are simple single colour designs with the remaining two thirds consisting of more elaborate decorations. The two countries' samples contained similar proportions of each. About one fifth of the plates had some gilding but this was much more prevalent in the British sample, reflecting the differences in tastes in the two countries discussed above. In decorated ware, decoration by lithographed transfer dominated, with hand decoration representing only a small proportion. Plates available in Germany were marginally more likely to be decorated by transfer but less likely to be hand decorated.

Turning to the more subjective characteristics, plates categorised for everyday use accounted for about 50% of the sample, while one-off purchases had the lowest share. Since the latter are most likely to comprise wedding or other gifts, this low share seems reasonable. Consumption of plates for everyday use represented a larger share of the German than the British sample. Finally branded products represented just under 50% of the total sample with international brands having a slightly higher share than national brands. There were differences across the two countries in this variable with national brands accounting for a greater proportion of the German sample. This again was consistent with the observations of buyers who suggested that German consumers were more likely to go for a known brand (preferably produced in Germany) whereas UK consumers were less concerned about where (by which manufacturer and geographically) the plates were produced.

Table B.2: Plate characteristics, design features

	Total		Britain		Germany	
	% of total sample	Average price (£)*	% of total sample	Average sample	% of total price (£)*	Average price (£)*
Total	100.0	9.75	100.0	10.28	100.0	8.70
Earthenware	35.9	6.30	43.2	6.21	19.3	6.69
Stoneware	7.7	6.84	9.2	6.82	4.8	6.91
Porcelain	42.2	10.29	29.4	12.33	66.9	8.55
Bone China	14.2	18.34	18.2	19.22	9.0	15.11
White	22.5	7.29	21.3	7.46	24.8	7.01
Plain	*12.9*	*7.12*	*12.1*	*7.41*	*14.5*	*6.64*
Embossed	*9.6*	*7.52*	*9.2*	*7.52*	*10.3*	*7.52*
Designed	77.5	10.46	78.7	11.05	75.2	9.26
Single design	25.1	9.34	24.5	10.10	26.2	7.94
Multi- design	*52.4*	*10.99*	*54.2*	*11.47*	*49.0*	*9.97*
Spray	20.1	5.79	22.6	5.82	15.2	5.71
Hand decorated	7.0	8.68	8.2	8.11	4.8	10.54
Transfer	50.4	12.57	47.9	14.02	55.2	10.12
Gilded	19.9	16.51	24.5	16.78	11.0	15.35
Everyday use	49.2	5.80	43.3	5.41	60.7	6.34
Stylish	34.6	11.44	41.5	11.95	21.4	9.55
Once in a lifetime	16.2	18.12	15.2	19.60	17.9	15.68
No Brand	55.5	6.48	60.0	6.76	46.9	5.80
National Brand	20.6	12.01	14.5	14.03	32.4	10.24
International Brand	23.9	15.37	25.5	16.41	20.7	12.87

For purposes of comparison German prices were converted to £ using the 1999 market exchange rate of 2.97 DM/£.

The average prices in the entire sample follow expected patterns across quality dimensions. Thus looking at body paste earthenware plates are cheapest with stoneware on average priced only marginally higher. Porcelain plates cost about 50% more on average than earthenware whereas the price premium for bone china is very large. White plates cost less than decorated and more elaborate designs are on average somewhat higher priced than more simple designs. Average prices of hand decorated and transfer printed plates are higher than spray and gilding appears to significantly add to the price. Plates which were deemed to be stylish or once off purchases on average cost more than those for everyday use and brand names appear to confer a substantial premium.

Comparisons of the absolute values of the British and German average price depends on the exchange rate used. But looking at each sub-group of characteristics relative to its base characteristic suggests there may be some differences in the two samples. Thus the difference between the average prices of porcelain and earthenware plates is proportionally lower in Germany than in Britain. Similar differences emerge when comparing transfer printed to spray and branded goods to those produced by manufacturers whose name is not considered to be synonymous with quality. The significance of these cross-country differences will be explored further below.

Looking at each quality variable in isolation conveys only a partial picture of how quality affects price because many of the variables are likely to be highly correlated with each other. An obvious example is bone china and gilding both of which dimensions have high average prices – gilding is most frequently placed on bone china plates. Also the significance of price differences across quality dimensions depends on the price variability which is large in our sample. Estimating the impact and significance of these variables requires the use of multiple regressions.

Hedonic regression results

The results of the hedonic regressions are shown in Table B.3. Equation 1 considers only the 'hard' characteristics. All coefficients are the expected positive sign. The results suggest, that other things equal, porcelain adds about 50% to price whereas bone china doubles it. Hand decoration and transfer printing also add significantly to price although by less than the body paste dimensions. The remaining variables are not significant at the 95% level.

Table B.3: Hedonic regression results. Dependent variable is log (price)

	equation (1)	equation (2)	equation(3)	equation (4) Whole sample coefficients	German coefficients
DU	1.40*	1.33*	1.28*	1.29*	
	(14.6)	(25.5)	(26.1)	(23.8)	
DG	2.29*	2.32*	2.23*	2.22*	
	(20.4)	(30.0)	(33.0)	(19.6)	
Stoneware	0.21	0.14	0.13	0.08	0.19
	(1.9)	(1.3)	(1.50)	(0.9)	(1.0)
Porcelain	0.49*	0.37*	0.23*	0.34*	-0.32*
	(6.2)	(5.3)	(3.60)	(4.7)	(2.2)
Bone china	1.05*	0.68*	0.41*	0.52*	-0.39*
	(11.4)	(7.7)	(5.16)	(5.3)	(2.4)
White embossed	0.05	-	-	-	-
	(0.5)				
Single design	0.05	-	-	-	-
	(0.4)				
Multi design	0.15	-	-	-	-
	(1.3)				
Gilded	0.11	0.04	0.10	0.11	-0.28
	(1.2)	(0.5)	(1.3)	(1.3)	(1.6)
Hand decorated	0.45*	0.24*	0.31*	0.24*	0.36
	(3.8)	(2.4)	(3.3)	(2.1)	(1.7)
Transfer	0.36*	0.27*	0.25*	0.20*	0.19
	(4.2)	(4.8)	(5.0)	(3.1)	(1.7)
Stylish	-	0.55*	0.42*	0.46*	-
		(10.0)	(7.6)	(7.6)	
One-off	-	0.75*	0.55*	0.62*	-
		(9.6)	(7.2)	(7.5)	
Brand-I	-	-	0.56*	0.43*	0.33*
			(9.2)	(5.8)	(2.7)
Brand N	-	-	0.48*	0.38*	0.25*
			(7.7)	(5.5)	(2.2)
adjusted R²	0.57	0.67	0.73	0.74	
No. observations	427		427	427	

Notes: absolute values of t-ratios in parentheses, standard errors are heteroskedastic consistent, * significant at 95% level. DU and DG are dummy variables for the UK and Germany, respectively. German coefficients are the quality dummies interacted with the German dummy variable and measure the extent to which the coefficients on these variables in the German sample differ from those in the UK.

Equation 2 adds the more subjective quality dimensions while omitting other variables such as white embossed, single and multi designs whose significance level was even further reduced when these new variables were added. Adding these new variables significantly increase the adjusted R^2 – in fact about 67% of the variance in prices can now be explained by these quality dimensions. All variables have the expected positive sign and none have a t-ratio less than 1. Equation 3 also adds brand as a variable. The proportionate impact on price of porcelain and bone china are much reduced in this third equation with high effects from brand name and the market to which they are aimed.

Finally we estimated equations allowing the characteristics to vary across the two countries by interacting the quality characteristics with the German dummy variable. The results are presented in equation 4 where very insignificant interaction variables (with t-ratios less than 1) were omitted. Adding these variables only marginally increases the adjusted R^2. Against this some of the individual interaction terms are significant. The coefficients on porcelain and bone are negative and significant suggesting these two types of body paste add proportionally less to price in Germany than in Britain when allowance is made for other variables. In fact the results suggest that porcelain, on its own, does not command a price premium in Germany. In contrast brand name commands a significantly greater premium in Germany than in Britain.

Table B.4 presents the estimated quality adjusted prices and PPPs from the above three regressions. Including the 'hard' characteristics alone gives a PPP somewhat below that found in the matched goods analysis discussed above. Adding the 'subjective' quality dimensions raises the PPP by about 5% but allowing the German coefficients to vary to an extent counterbalances this so that the end result is a PPP only marginally lower than that derived from the matched plate approach.

Table B.4: Estimated average quality adjusted prices and PPPs

	UK price(£)	German price (DM)	PPP
Equation 1	4.05	9.89	2.44
Equation 2	3.80	10.14	2.67
Equation 3	3.61	9.26	2.57
Equation 4	3.62	9.16	2.53

It is useful to consider how sensitive the PPP calculations are to minor variations in the regression equations. To do we ran a number of regressions adding or deleting variables to get some idea of how specific variables affect relative PPPs. The first set of experiments began by setting as a base an equation including body paste and whether the plate was white or designed – these 'hard' quality dimensions are considered to be fundamental. We then added each of the individual variables in turn. The second base category was equation 2 above and the experiment deleted each variable other than the body paste categories in turn. The third experiment again began with equation 2 but added one German interaction variable at a time. Finally the fourth experiment used equation 3 as a base and deleted a German interactive variable from each regression. The results showed average PPPs over the experiments close to those presented in Table B.4 with generally low standard deviations relative to the mean suggesting the results are reasonably robust to the equation specifications.

These experiments did however suggest that some individual variables are important. The main culprits are national brand and the German porcelain and bone china interactive variables. In the case of the interactive variables it makes little sense in an equation to include or exclude these two variables alone since other interactive variables are also significant. The relatively large impact of national brand is a bit more worrying if this variable is not in fact a good signal for quality. Omitting both brand variables from equation 2 would raise the estimated PPP to 2.66 DM/£, an increase of 3.5% over the base equation 2 estimate. However excluding these two variables also significantly lowers the explanatory power of the regression. If some part of the brand name premium captures elements of market power enjoyed by the brand name manufacturers, then the PPPs for equations 2 and 3 above are likely to be (marginally) biased downwards.

Results: Quality rankings

We now turn to a consideration of the results of the quality rankings method which attempts to take account directly of difficult to observe quality dimensions rather than rely on proxy variables such as brand name. This analysis was based on a sub sample of the prices collected for the hedonic regression analysis and primarily consisted of plates shown to one or more retail buyer. But some additional observations were added which the researchers believed had characteristics typical of the group. This was particularly the case for plates in the basic category whose lack of quality attributes was reasonably transparent. Without adding some more observations the sample sizes in the categories would have been unreliable.   Thus calculations were based on a sample of 28 price quotations in the top group, 31 in the superior group, 33 in the standard group and 23 in the basic group.

Table B.5 shows the average prices and PPPs by quality grade. As stated above these are weighted averages of white and decorated plates. In both countries top quality plates command prices nearly double those in the Superior quality which in turn commands about a 50% premium on standard quality plates. Basic quality plates were found to be significantly cheaper relative to standard plates in Britain than in Germany. Thus the PPP was higher for basic quality than for the remaining three grades. The overall PPP is calculated by weighting the PPPs in each category by their market shares in each country and then taking the geometric mean of the two.[81] This results in a quality equivalent PPP of 2.34 DM/£ which is some 7.5% lower than the matched plate comparison or that based on equation 3 of the hedonic regressions. Thus allowing in this more direct method for a whole range of quality dimensions leads to a larger adjustment in favour of higher quality in Germany.

Table B.5: Quality gradings: Prices, market shares and PPPs

Quality grading	Average prices by quality-grade			Market share (% total domestic sales)	
	UK (£)	D (DM)	PPP	UK	D
Top	21.42	47.25	2.21	10	20
Superior	11.33	25.41	2.24	30	40
Standard	7.31	16.29	2.23	30	25
Basic	3.01	8.23	2.74	30	15
TOTAL				100	100

Ratio of UK to German prices using:
A. UK market share weights	2.38
B. German market share weights	2.31
Geometric mean of A and B	2.34

The resulting price ratios were subjected to statistical tests to see how robust they were to inclusion or deletion of plates in the various categories and for small changes in the weighting schemes, both overall categories and ratios of white to decorated plates. The results were found to be reasonably robust to these tests – the overall PPP did not change by more than 5% in any the alternatives.[82]

B.3 Production price ratios

As outlined in the main text, the consumption PPPs were employed in the calculations of relative productivity on the grounds that adjustments to a production price ratio basis were either unnecessary or unreliable. This section outlines the analysis which led us to this conclusion. It first considers the issue of possible adjustments for distribution margins and then recalculates price ratios on a 'production basis' using all four methods.

Adjustment for distribution margins
In three of the four methods, in order to calculate the production price it is desirable to adjust the price ratios for differences in retail margins in the two countries. Information on margins are available for the two countries from their retail trade inquiries[83]. These are available for two categories, specialist household goods stores and department stores. In the UK the ratio of gross margin to sales was 40.2 and 31.6 respectively for the two categories, comparable figures for Germany were 38.7 and 20.3. Hence taken separately retail margins were higher in the UK but in both countries specialist retailers had higher margins than Department stores. Combining the shares of sales through the two types of outlets, assuming specialist stores account for 85% of German and 12% of British sales, with the retail margins listed above yield an estimate of aggregate German retail margins 9% higher than in Britain.[84]

This may not be an appropriate adjustment in the context of the data used in this report which were largely price quotations from Department/Variety stores in both countries. Comparing retail margins in the two countries for this category of retail outlet alone yields an estimate of 38% higher margins in Britain. However this is not a valid comparison since discussions with retail buyers suggested that Department stores in the UK purchase ceramic tableware primarily direct from firms whereas German Department stores purchase mainly from wholesale distributors. In 1998 the wholesale margin in Germany for non-electrical household goods manufactured from metals and ceramics was 33.6%.[85] Combining this estimate with the retail margins for German department stores suggest total trade margins less than 3% lower than in Britain.

On balance we conclude that trade margins are probably not very different in the two countries when applied to the sample of plate prices used in this report. Given that information on margins is available only for broadly defined retail groups and not ceramic tableware specifically, we decided it was best not to include any adjustment for trade margins.

Unit value ratios and matched plates

This is the one method where allowance is not needed for retail margins since sales are valued at producer prices. The method is identical to that used to calculate consumption unit values with manufacturers values and quantities replacing consumption figures. The production unit value ratio for 1999 was calculated at 3.45 DM/£ which again seems very high. But for the reasons given above this method is considered to be the least reliable of the four and so can largely be ignored. In this case of matched plates only three third country imports were excluded so the bulk of the sample was retained. The result was only a marginal change in the matched plate comparison from a consumption PPP of 2.55 DM/£ to a 'production' price ratio of 2.5DM/£.

Hedonic regressions

This analysis was carried out on plates produced either in the UK or Germany. The sample size was reduced to 256 plates of which 151 were produced in the UK and 105 in Germany. The smaller sample size implied that some variables had a very small number of observations, notably stoneware and hand decorated plates. Stoneware was removed as a separate variable so that the base category in terms of body paste was earthenware and stoneware combined. Hand decoration was added to transfer. Similarly some of the interaction variables resulted in the too few observations on Germany alone and remaining variables such as German national brand were very highly

Table B.6: Hedonic regression results, UK or German products.
Dependent variable is log (price)

	equation (1)	equation(2)
DU	1.79*	1.50*
	(15.7)	(23.9)
DG	2.63*	2.44*
	(20.3)	(34.1)
Porcelain	0.32*	0.05
	(3.42)	(0.7)
Bone china	0.72*	0.29*
	(6.6)	(3.3)
White embossed	-0.04	-
	(0.3)	
Single design	0.02	-
	(0.1)	
Multi design	0.01	-
	(0.0)	
Gilded	0.23*	0.16*
	(2.2)	(2.0)
Hand/Transfer	0.31	0.26*
	(3.0)	(4.7)
Stylish	-	0.21*
		(3.5)
One-off	-	0.37*
		(5.3)
Brand-I	-	0.60*
		(8.9)
Brand N	-	0.51*
		(7.9)
adjusted R²	0.58	0.75
No. observations	256	256

Notes: absolute values of t-ratios in parentheses, standard errors are heterocedastic consistent, * significant at 95% level.

correlated with the German country dummy. For these reasons it was only equations 1 and 2 were estimated for the restricted sample. The coefficient estimates in Table B.6 appear to be somewhat different than those in Table B.3. The chief difference is that the quality adjusted prices in both countries are higher than in the original regressions but this is hardly surprising as generally cheaper third country imports are excluded from both samples. The coefficients on the body paste terms, method by which the decoration was applied and the stylish/one-off variables are all lower whereas those on gilding, and brand names are higher. Despite these differences the overall performance of the equations are similar as confirmed by standard F-tests. In equation 1 the estimated PPP was 2.32 DM/£ whereas in equation 2 it was 2.56DM/3. In the latter case, which on statistical grounds is the preferred specification, there is no significant between the quality adjusted PPPs in the restricted sample relative to the entire sample.

Quality rankings

In the case of the quality rankings method, deleting all non British or German produced products yielded a price ratio of 2.24 DM/£, about 4% lower than the consumption price ratio using this method. But this left very few observations in the basic category – there are very few if any German producers at this level.

In summary the experiments attempting to calculate production rather than consumption price ratios of ceramic tableware, comparing Germany with Britain, either yielded results which were close to consumption price ratios or were based on unreliable methods. Hence the estimated consumption PPPs were employed in evaluating real productivity differences in the two countries.

Notes

[71] For example the unit value method has been applied in B. van Ark, *International Comparisons of Output and Productivity: Manufacturing Productivity Performance in Ten Countries from 1950 to 1990*, Groningen Growth and Development Centre, Monograph series No. 1, 1993, and M. O'Mahony, *Britain's Relative Productivity Performance: An International Perspective*, National Institute of Economic and Social Research, London, 1999.

[72] In one visit to the UK factory we witnessed a multi-coloured floral design with writing being applied by bomb-printing.

[73] We also experimented with other characteristics such as whether the design was original or an imitation but were unable to satisfactorily divide the sample along these lines.

[74] This was the average of final quarter 1999 and first quarter 2000. *Source: National Institute Economic Review, 3/2000.*

[75] Data for the UK were taken from *PRA27 Household & Miscellaneous Ceramics, Product Sales and Trade, Ceramic Household and Ornamental Articles, 26210*, ONS 1999 and for Germany from *Europroms: EU production and trade Statisitics*, Eurostat.

[76] Frequently in exercises of this kind, researchers need to be concerned by 'retail noise', i.e. the same products being charged at different rates in different stores. In fact this generally did not arise in Britain; identical plates were sold at the same price both across stores and across regions. In Germany there was more variation across retail outlets for identical plates, although these also accounted for a minority of observations. In cases of more than one price for the same plate, we averaged over the observations.

[77] Mintel: *Market Intelligence Report: China and Earthenware*, May 1998.

[78] Some manufacturers produce a 'plate series' where the price is the same but each plate has a minor variation, e.g. blue rim on white and yellow rim on white. Only one of these observations was included.

[79] The unbalanced size of the sample in the two countries reflects their differing retail distribution systems. Department stores are more prevalent in the UK whereas German consumers are more likely to purchase goods in specialist stores – it was more difficult to obtain a large number of price quotations from the latter.

[80] The value shares (the sum over body paste types of price multiplied by quantity divided by total sales) are not generally consistent with aggregate shares as given in Table 2 of the main text. Hence the average price for the sample should not be seen as an estimate of average consumption prices; a more reliable estimate of this was calculated above. Rather the numbers at best give an indication of the proportionate price premiums of one category over another.

[81] It is easy to show that weighting by UK value shares is equivalent to ratio of the sum (over gradings) of UK prices multiplied by UK quantities over the sum of German prices multiplied by UK quantities.

[82] At an early stage of the analysis some plates were excluded or moved between categories as their contribution to the overall PPP amounted to too high a proportion (the criterion used was to exclude or move to an adjacent group if the plate price was more than twice or less than half the average for the group).

[83] UK, from *Services Sector Survey: Retail Trade*, 1998, ONS; Germany: from Binnenhandel, Gastgewerbe, Tourismus, Fachserie 6, Reihe 3.2. *Beschäftigung, Umsatz, Wareneingang, Lagerbestand und Investitionen im Einzelhandel, 1999*, Statistisches Bundesamt, Wiesbaden.

[84] Sales shares by outlet for the UK were taken from Mintel: *Market Intelligence Report: China and Earthenware*. May 1998. Estimates for Germany were based on discussions with retail buyers; this is consistent with data for all household given in Retail Intelligence, *Retailing in Germany, Corporate Intelligence Report*, London, 2000.

[85] *Binnenhandel, Gastgewrbe, Tourismus, Fachserie 6, Reihe 1.2, Beschäftigung, Umsatz, Wareneingang, Lagerbestand und Investitionen im Grobhandel, 1998*, Statistisches Bundesamt, Wiesbaden.

Appendix C

Firm samples compared with national population data

Official data on establishment sizes are no longer published for the UK, and have not been since the 1992 Revision to the Standard Industrial Classification - giving data at the level of the *tableware* industry (rather than the *ceramic goods* sector) - was carried out. Such data are available for Germany, together with earlier computations available on a similar basis to Britain (ie, at the level of the ceramics producing sector as a whole) and show a similar spread of establishment sizes (or, at least that central band of employment which constitutes the inter-quartile range) in both cases. In seeking to assess the representativeness of our sample, we combined these disparate sources for comparison with the plant sizes typically encountered in our sample.

Table C.1: Distribution of national plant sizes in ceramics and tableware industries

| | Ceramic goods industry, 1994 [a] | | Tableware [b] |
	UK	Germany	Germany, 1995
<100	22	15	16
100-199	12	13	11
200-499	33	35	39
500-999	18	28	34
1000+	<u>15</u>	<u>11</u>	....
	100	100	100
Total employment	42,800	44,074	21,443
Lower quartile	143	180	183
Median	345	399	392
Upper quartile	784	737	633

[a] Figures refer to the ceramics goods industry as a whole (in the UK: SIC_{80} 2489 ceramic goods; in Germany, $Sypro_{79}$ nr. 51 *Feinkeramik)*, and include workers engaged in, for example, the production of sanitaryware, tiles and slabs. [b] Figures refer to those engaged in the production of household ceramics (SIC_{92} 2621).*Sources*: for the UK: Central Statistics Office, *PA1003 Size distribution of UK businesses 1994*, Table 8; for Germany: Statistisches Bundesamt, *Produzierendes Gewerbe Fachserie 4 Reihe 4.1.2 Betriebe, Beschäftigte und Umsatz im Bergbau und im Verabeitenden Gewerbe nach Beschäftigtengrößenklassen 1994* and *1995* Tables 1.1, 1.2 and 2.1. some 17 *plants* visited in Britain, 13 in Germany, these plants in fact represented some 12 *firms* in the UK, 11 in Germany. For the sake of completeness, and for the avoidance of doubt as to the degree of comparability of our two countries' samples, Table C2 provides an alternative disaggregation of firm-sizes on the basis of the *combined employment* for each of the plants visited *per firm*.

Table C.1 summarises the size distribution of manufacturing plants in the broader ceramic sector in the two countries, together with the distribution of plants visited in the course of this inquiry. The reader will note that the average German plant engaged in ceramics manufacturing is only slightly larger than the average British plant, at 399 compared to 345 employees, though with a slightly narrower inter-quartile range of establishments covering the central half of employment-sizes in the two countries sizes in Germany (180-737 employees) compared to Britain (143-784 employees).

With such similarities between the distributions of the wider ceramics sector clearly apparent, we felt reasonably confident in relying on the German data to provide closer estimates of actual size distribution of 'local units' in the national populations.

In Table 5 of the main text, we present a breakdown of the sample firms visited by employment-size *for each of the individual plants visited.* However, as we say in the text, it is not uncommon to find manufacturers organising the various production activities *across several specialised sites,* so that the forming and decorating activities may be spread among a number of manufacturing plants; or organising production of different types in different 'local units'. This complication means that while our sample consisted of some 17 *plants* visited in Britain, 13 in Germany, these plants in fact represented some 12 *firms* in the UK, 11 in Germany. For the sake of completeness, and for the avoidance of doubt as to the degree of comparability of our two countries' samples, Table C.2 provides an alternative disaggregation of firm-sizes on the basis of the *combined employment* for each of the plants visited *per firm.*

Table C.2: Distribution of sample firm sizes: combined plant-level employment from each of the firms visited: UK and Germany, 1999-2000

	UK		Germany	
	No firms visited	% share of employment	No firms visited	% share of employment
<200	2	5	1	3
200-499	4	29	6	39
500+	6	66	4	58
	12	100	11	100
Total employment	5,260		4,541	
Plant average	438		413	